# West Cork Walks

*Including*
*Lee Valley, Mountain*
*& Coastal Regions*

*Text and Illustrations*
## KEVIN CORCORAN

THE O'BRIEN PRESS
DUBLIN

First published 1991 by The O'Brien Press Ltd,
20 Victoria Road, Dublin 6, Ireland.
Tel +353 1 4923333 Fax +353 1 4922777
E-mail books@obrien.ie
Website www.obrien.ie
Reprinted 1991. Revised editions 1996, 1999. This revised edition 2005.

ISBN 0-86278-928-1

British Library Cataloguing in Publication Data
Corcoran, Kevin
West Cork Walks. - 4th ed.
1.Walking - Ireland - Cork - Guidebooks
2.Cork (Ireland : County) - Guidebooks
I.Title
914.1'95'04824

5 6 7 8 9 10
05 06 07 08

Typesetting, editing, design and layout: The O'Brien Press
Printing: Cox & Wyman Ltd

The walks in this book have been designed to ensure comfortable access to the countryside with due consideration to land owners. Rights-of-way were followed and sought where possible; however, the fact that a walk is outlined in this book is no guarantee of a recognised right of way.

Land ownership and conditions can change, and where problems do arise the author would appreciate such changes being brought to his attention so that future editions can be modified. The author and the publishers do not accept any responsibility where trespass may occur, neither do they accept any responsibility for accident or loss by the public when carrying out these walks. Common sense should prevail at all times. Take the advice of locals and heed all warning signs.

On NO account should dogs be brought on any of these walks as they cause annoyance and disturbance to livestock, wildlife and to other members of the public. Show respect for the countryside, as the irresponsible actions of one person can destroy the enjoyment of so many others.

# West Cork Walks

West Cork covers the entire area from the long winding coast in the south between Kinsale and Kerry, up through Dunmanway to Macroom, and on through Ballyvourney to the adjacent Kerry border at the northern end.

To the naturalist this forms a complete terrain, as one can follow the borderline of rocky sandstone outcrops and concomitant Lusitanian flora that mark it out. Here one will find a constancy of topography and of wildlife characteristics, well documented by the botanist Robert Lloyd Praeger.

It is an extensive area, ideal for the casual explorer, where the wilds are readily accessible with relatively little effort.

Access to the northern part of West Cork is easiest through Macroom on the river Lee, and to the southern part through Bandon on the river Bandon.

'An expert and informative book. Kevin Corcoran is an environmental biologist and a dab hand at drawing.'
MICHAEL VINEY, THE IRISH TIMES

'This book provides a revealing insight into one of the most beautiful parts of the country.'
EVENING PRESS

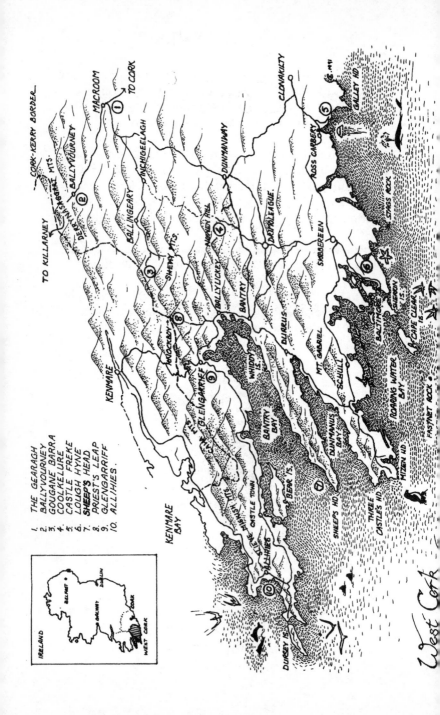

IRELAND

BELFAST

GALWAY • DUBLIN

CORK
WEST CORK

1. THE GEARAGH
2. BALLYVOURNEY
3. GOUGANE BARRA
4. COOLKELURE
5. CASTLE FREKE
6. LOUGH HYNE
7. SHEEP'S HEAD
8. PRIEST'S LEAP
9. GLENGARRIFF
10. ALLIHIES.

West Cork

TO CORK
CORK-KERRY BORDER
TO KILLARNEY
MACROOM
① 
② BALLYVOURNEY
DERRYNASAGGART MTS.
BALLINGEARY
INCHIGEELAGH
③
SHEHY MTS.
⑧
KNOCKBOY
KENMARE
⑨
GLENGARRIFF
CALHA MTS.
KENMARE BAY
THE MISKISH MTS.
ALLIHIES
⑩
DURSEY IS.
CASTLE TOWN
BERE IS.
BANTRY BAY
WHIDDY IS.
BANTRY
DURRUS
MT. GABRIEL
SCHULL
SHEEP'S HD.
DUNMANUS BAY
THREE CASTLES HD.
MIZEN HD.
FASTNET ROCK.
CAPE CLEAR
ROARING WATER BAY
BALTIMORE
SHERKIN IS.
CLEAR IS.
SKIBBEREEN
LOUGH INE
⑥
STAGS ROCK
ROSS CARBERY
GALLEY HD.
MT.
CLONAKILTY
DUNMANWAY
GLANDORE
④ NOWEN HILL
COOLKELURE
BALLYVICKEY
DRINAGH

# Contents

*All walks are circular except No. 8, Priest's Leap*

DEDICATION
*To Ragleth*

# Introduction

The rugged landscape of West Cork, with its wondrous mix of mountains and their expansive tracts of moor, its wild hills full of lakes and tarns, the deep river valleys cloaked with occasional remnants of aboriginal oak, its hedgerowed farms stretched across hilly pastures of thin peat and its heavily indented coastline of cliffed promontories, must be one of the most magical places in Ireland to wander in. A country that has existed since before the formation of the mighty Alps and Himalayas, it presents a terrain that has been wrinkled and buckled by time into a thousand shapes. Thus it holds a multitude of wild corners within which a rich human and wildlife heritage can still survive relatively intact. Furthermore, being the most southerly point of the country ensures that it gets the full benefit of the warming Gulf Stream that caresses its shores. This, along with the sheltered aspect of its many deep-valleyed mountain ranges confers an assemblage of characteristics on the region that are unsurpassed by any other part of the Eurasian land mass.

Although rich in folklore and history there are other aspects to the region that are as yet not fully appreciated. The wild inhospitable nature of much of its topography has provided a welcome haven for an extensive cross-section of native wildlife. Here they thrive in the expansive tracts of wilderness that also have survived relatively undisturbed up to now. Plants from another time litter the bogs, mountain slopes and old meadows – to such an extent that over a quarter of all the rare Irish plants can be found in West Cork and its neighbouring South Kerry. The south-west acts as the Irish headquarters for many of our more interesting plants, such as the strange Lusitanians, a group of plants not generally found elsewhere in either Europe or Britain, apart from a small corner of northern Portugal. These are possible survivors from before the Ice Age and no one knows how they arrived in Ireland. Most of Ireland's other species came by colonisation ten thousand years ago across the land bridges that once linked Ireland, England and the Continent. Speculation leads to the idea that perhaps there was a land bridge between Ireland and Portugal about two million years ago when the Lusitanians originated. There is no evidence to support this of course, and the origin of the Lusitanians remains shrouded in mystery.

For its bird life, West Cork must be one of the best places in all of

Western Europe to watch for passing migrants. Additionally, it is also the best place in Europe to see whales as they pass up and down along the west coast migrating annually between their feeding grounds in the Arctic and their breeding quarters in the equatorial regions, while the many off-shore islands and pinnacled rocks contain very significant breeding colonies of internationally important species.

Sadly, the entire fabric of this incredible wealth is now under considerable threat. Modern progress, driven by an enormous level of greed and stupefying ignorance, marches across the entire region as it has already done over the greater portion of the rest of Europe. This beautiful coastline is marred by the horrible sprawl of bungalow blight, the few remaining woods seem to compel some individuals to an immediate bout of tree-felling, the priceless bogs are being pointlessly destroyed in the belief that they can be turned into fertile green fields, the hedgerows are being bulldozed out of existence, turning the farmland into sterile green deserts, and the lakes and rivers are used as dumping grounds for all sorts of rubbish and effluent. The south-west represents one of the last few strongholds of extensive wilderness left in western Europe, but it is now being raped with such alarming rapidity that quite soon Ireland too will have lost one of its last great assets as a tourist destination.

Thus the intention of this book is to introduce, inform, educate and share with as many people as possible the real beauty of our unique countryside in the hope that if enough people appreciate what we have got, a strong, well-informed public opinion may be the last means by which to save it. If 'development' is left to its own devices, very soon there will be nothing left to protect.

## THE WALKS

The walks have been designed to introduce the walker to this wild and threatened heritage in as safe a manner as possible, with the bulk of them being accessible to all types. Moving through the various habitats that are found in West Cork, you will come to know the occupants of these diminishing communities, of their fragile existence and the forces that now threaten them. From woods, mountain, bog, farmland, beach, cliff, dune, to fresh-water lake and river, you can visit them all at different seasons of the year and their significance is illustrated and explained. I have no doubt that they will draw you out again and again to experience the delights of an ever-changing landscape. However, just because these areas have been outlined in the book it is not realistic to assume that there will be no danger involved. Thus when visiting the various areas it is important to remember a number of points as outlined below.

## DANGER

Common sense and discretion should always be used when in the wilderness, especially if you are not familiar with the ways of the countryside. Please take note of the following points.

*Mountains*: The higher peaks are prone to rapidly descending fogs and mists which will make it impossible to descend safely, thus attempt these only on fine clear days when there is no threat of rain and its accompanying low cloud. The walks that are generally affected by this are Nos.3 (Gougane) and 10 (Allihies), and to a lesser extent No.8 (The Priest's Leap – OPTION) and No.7 (Sheep's Head).

*Cliffs*: These should be treated with the greatest of respect, especially in wet and windy weather when they can be prone to erosion and instant collapse. Keep your distance from them and on no account allow children free rein near them. The walk affected is No. 7 (Sheep's Head).

*Waves*: There is such a thing as a freak wave that thunders onto the shore during wild and windy weather. These can turn up irregularly every fifteen to twenty-five minutes, depending on the swell. Most people like to get near the crashing waves on a headland or a rock, measuring their safety distance by the immediate waves observed. Tragically, many lives have been lost over the years as unwary visitors have been caught by a sudden and unexpected enormous freak wave. The walks affected are Nos. 5 (Castlefreke) and 10 (Allihies).

*Mine shafts*: Much mining occurred around the coastline of West Cork in the last century, and this left a large number of abandoned mine shafts. Obviously these are frighteningly dangerous and should not be treated lightly. Although most are crudely fenced off there is still the possibility of danger, especially if they have been interfered with, so keep your distance from them. The walk affected is No. 10 (Allihies).

*Rights-of-way*: As far as was possible all the routes in this book follow recognised rights-of-way and across commonages. However, in some cases it was not possible to fully discern this and the land may undergo a change of ownership. Avoid trespass, but in general most landowners are reasonable as long as you respect their property and they are treated with the courtesy they deserve. If difficulties do arise, please be discreet and leave the property promptly but safely (and the author would appreciate the point being brought to his attention). For your own benefit and that of other walkers, DO NOT BRING DOGS, as they worry cattle and sheep.

*Poison*: On no account should any plants described in the book be tasted or eaten, as many are poisonous and can cause severe if not fatal illness.

*Clothing*: Wear good boots that have a reasonably good grip. Wet and cold weather can occur at any time of the year, thus you should dress accordingly. It is better to wear several layers of warm clothing than one thick garment as layers can be taken off and put on depending on conditions. For this purpose it is very handy to have some form of knapsack that leaves your hands free.

*Litter*: Please take all your litter home with you and dispose of it sensibly – become part of the solution, not the problem!

## USING THE BOOK

The text is ideally meant to be read in conjunction with the walk, but it is a good idea to read through the entire walk before you set out. Each walk is divided into numbered sections, and these numbers are marked on the accompanying map. Use the map regularly to check your location. Starting at point number one, follow the dotted line on to point number two and so on throughout the route. If you lose your bearings at any time, try to find your position on the map and refer to the previous numbered point, which should explain your next move.

## WALK DESCRIPTIONS AND CHARACTERISTICS

*Distances*: All distances are given for the round trip with the extra distance for the OPTIONS given separately.

*Time*: This is given as an approximate minimum for the completion of the round trip. Obviously this will vary greatly for the type of people involved and the amount of time they spend stopping and exploring. On average give yourself half an hour per mile on the casual walks but an hour to the mile for the strenuous ones, adding on as much time as you like for rests, picnics and so on. In winter be careful of the early sunset and the inevitable darkness which can occur from 16.30 onwards – set out early!

| WALK | HABITAT | LENGTH | TIME | SUITABILITY |
|---|---|---|---|---|
| The Gearagh | wetland and drowned forest | 4ml/ 6.5km | 2hrs | casual, suited to all, but floods in heavy rains |
| Ballyvourney | woodland and country lanes | 7.5ml/ 12km | 3.5hrs | casual, suited to all |
| Gougane Barra | mountain peaks and upland heath | 6ml/ 10km | 4 hrs | strenuous, needs clear weather, climbing experience necessary |
| Coolkelure | country road amidst rocky hills and farms | 5.5ml/ 9km | 2.5hrs | very casual, suited to all |
| Castlefreke | beach, dunes and old demesne | 5.5ml/ 9km | 3hrs OPTION 0.5hrs | very casual, suited to all |
| Lough Hyne | marine lake and old woods | 4ml/ 6.5km | 2.5hrs | casual, suited to all |
| Sheep's Head | cliffed coastline and heathland | 10ml/ 16km | 7hrs+ | tough, for the fit |
| Priest's Leap | glaciated valley and mountain peak | 5.5ml/ 8.8km OPTION 2.5ml/ 4km | 3hrs OPTION 1hr | moderate, for the fit |
| Glengarriff | oak and conifer woods | 5ml/ 8km | 3hrs | very casual, suited to all |
| Allihies | coastal mountain, bogland and beach | 7ml/ 10km | 4hrs | strenuous, needs clear weather |

# 1 – The Gearagh

THE RIVER LEE IS THE LARGEST RIVER in Ireland's extreme south-west, and was formed and shaped by extensive glaciers that covered the region during the last Ice Age. Rising high in the uplands of West Cork, the river experiences many changes before emptying into the tidal waters of Cork harbour. Tumbling down over waterfall and cascade, through deep gorges, expansive lakes and wooded plains, it is, to say the least, an incredibly beautiful river, and was once one of Ireland's most valuable salmon nurseries.

But there is no more fascinating region along its length than that open stretch of water near the town of Macroom, called the Gearagh. Today a sizable reservoir, it was until the 1950s a post-glacial, alluvial oak river-forest. Here was a place where time itself had stood still. Up to the 1950s the Gearagh had remained unchanged since its formation ten thousand years previously, at the end of the last Ice Age. Woefully, vast sections of this aboriginal forest were drowned by the rising waters caused by the Lee hydroelectric scheme.

It is hard to imagine what the area looked like before being flooded – a vast inland delta of inter-connecting, many-branched streams that encircled a maze of small and inaccessible islands, covered in oak forest. It was protected from the ravages of humanity by its swampy terrain, deep swirling streams and treacherous banks of soft muds with holes big enough to swallow a horse. Furthermore, the maze of channels became a nightmare to the unacquainted, causing them to experience the frightening phenomenon of *mescán mearaí* or 'confused direction', where a person kept going around in circles, finding it impossible to get out! This was a fate meted out to many a past arm of the law when trying to catch illegal *poitín* makers and outlaws who found sanctuary there, none more famous than the seventeenth-century Robin Hood-style character Seán Rua na Gaoire, 'Red-haired Sean of the Gearagh'.

On first sight, the Gearagh can appear barren and desolate. Like some lunar-type landscape, its wide expanse of water and mud, punctured by an army of blackened oak stumps, stretches across the flat-bottomed valley. Bleak and forlorn, as if scarred by the aftermath of some great war or fireball, the Gearagh National Nature Reserve appears lonely and uninviting. Yet if you venture to explore this strange landscape, you will be pleasantly surprised by the incredible wealth of wildlife there. Even though the flooding necessitated the felling of the entire area to give us its present appearance, nature as always fights back. The isolation and remoteness of this wet wonderland offers a welcome haven for much of Ireland's fast-diminishing flora and fauna. Because the Gearagh was left to nature after being flooded, and not further tampered with, many of the plant species that had formerly occupied the ancient forest began to re-emerge from seed, recolonising the marshy tracts and severed islands. Newly formed lagoons became sanctuaries for rare aquatic species that were being destroyed elsewhere, while the broad sheets of shallow water became a haven for migrant fowl, whose natural habitats are being vandalised by modern agriculture, industrial waste and ignorant developments. Defiantly, the trees too have begun to re-colonise the islands at the top of the reservoir, to form a water-locked, swampy woodland.

We have thus been given a second chance to protect the last fragment of our once extensive post-glacial, alluvial forests that cloaked much of the island of Ireland and a large part of mainland Europe, before the arrival of humans. It is imperative that the Gearagh be protected from any further abuse, such as indiscriminate tourism and bungalow developments. Hopefully we have learned our mistake and will take up the challenge.

## WALK DESCRIPTION

LOCATION: 3ml/5km from the town of Macroom, on the Inchigeelagh-Bantry road, which branches off the main Macroom-Cork road (on the Cork side of Macroom). Proceed along the reservoir's northern shoreline until the small but obvious gateway/lay-by is met on the left. You can park here. The gateway leads out to the picturesque stone bridges on the causeway that runs across the length of the lake.

TERRAIN: A casual walk through country lanes and quiet by-roads that cross the drowned forest. NOTE: In winter the causeway occasionally becomes submerged during prolonged spells of wet weather, when the reservoir fills to capacity and the walk becomes inaccessible. During the summer months this happens less often.

FEATURES: Ancient Ice Age forest remains; rich flora and fauna; drowned settlement; national nature reserve; swampy fen; country lanes; rare plants; extensive colonies of birds.

LENGTH: 4ml/6.5km.

TIME: 2 hours.

EQUIPMENT: Walking boots or wellingtons; light, wind-proof jacket; binoculars an advantage.

NOTE: Please do not bring dogs onto the reserve as they cause considerable annoyance to nesting birds and young chicks. You should also be aware of the fact that a number of shooting interests have dogmatically retained the right to carry out an annual slaughter of the wild birds during the winter months. This may be extremely upsetting for the more educated visitor to the reserve and you should consult local hotels if you wish to avoid this.

## WALK OUTLINE

(1) On arriving at the gateway proceed directly onto the causeway that leads out across the water. This is the old quarry road built at the turn of the century to take out the limestone found on the opposite side. It leads across the reservoir, via the stone bridges, passing the now drowned quarry and its abandoned settlement. Fine views of the outline of the former forest can be had from the bridges. The forest covered the entire

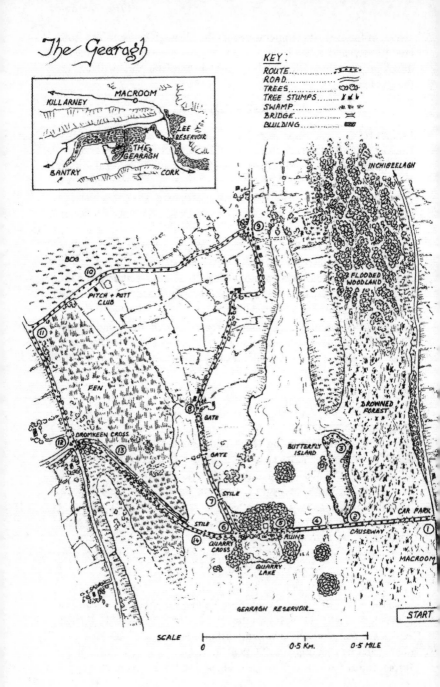

The Gearagh

KEY:
ROUTE............
ROAD............
TREES...........
TREE STUMPS.......
SWAMP...........
BRIDGE..........
BUILDING.........

KILLARNEY    MACROOM
LEE RESERVOIR
BANTRY    THE GEARAGH    CORK

INCHIGEELAGH

BOG

PITCH + PUTT CLUB

FLOODED WOODLAND

DROWNED FOREST

FEN

GATE

DROMKEEN CROSS

GATE

BUTTERFLY ISLAND

STILE

STILE

QUARRY CROSS

RUINS

CAR PARK

CAUSEWAY

MACROOM

QUARRY LAKE

GEARAGH RESERVOIR

START

SCALE
0        0·5 KM.        0·5 MILE

14

valley floor, hemmed in by the long, hilly ridges of Sleveen to the north and Toons to the south.

When the reservoir is very low, you will notice the many islands that were inaccessible due to the maze of streams that surrounded them, now covered with decapitated tree trunks. Additionally, during the summer, the muddy surfaces of these islands are smothered in a short, green growth that looks very like moss. This is in fact an extremely rare plant called *mudwort*, with 90 percent of the plant's population being found in the Gearagh. The remaining 10 percent is found near a small turlough in County Clare. However, if the reservoir is partly full the most you will see is the tops of the tree stumps projecting above the water, especially if it has been raining.

Mudwort – not found in West Cork prior to the drowning of the forest. This rare and diminishing plant has found a new life-saving home in the Gearagh.

(2) After the third bridge, a little causeway on your RIGHT leads to a small island. Walk onto this and follow its shoreline around in an anti-clockwise direction. In summer it is full of wild flowers and grasses such as the yellow *hawkweeds*, purple *mints* and tall *fescues*, and is very reminiscent of the old hay meadows that existed before the advent of modern intensive farming. Thus it attracts a lot of the butterflies that are common in the Gearagh, especially the *whites*, *tortoise-shells*, *peacocks* and *meadow browns*, which can occur in such large numbers during peak reproductive periods that the meadows shimmer with their movements. This is why it has been nicknamed 'butterfly island' by local children.

(3) The walk around this wild meadow also brings you very close to the many islands that are crowned with the grotesque shapes of twisted and blackened oak stumps. In between lie deep, muddy channels, choked with white *lily* cups and their plate-like leaves, and underneath the streams are filled with the treacherous tangle of abandoned branches

left behind after the forest was felled. These channels now provide the ideal hiding place for gigantic *pike*, some reaching lengths of 1.5m.

Hidden amongst the oak stumps on the islands are inconspicuous mounds of stones, now the only remains of the once thriving *poitá¡án* stills. But you are more likely to see the many grey *herons* that stand sentry-like on the stumps, watching for the shoals of *minnow* and *stickleback* that inhabit the shallows. If you have the time, this is an excellent place to hide amongst the tall grasses to watch for *kingfishers*, *grebes* and *duck* that ply up and down along the many channels. In the late evening you may be lucky enough to see an *otter*.

(4) On returning to the main causeway go RIGHT and follow the stony track. This was once a tarred road, but the surface has since been washed away by the fluctuating water levels. In summer, if you look across over the water, you will notice how the air above comes alive with skimming flocks of *swallow*, *martin* and *swift* as they feed upon the swarms of insects emerging from the relatively unpolluted water. From April onwards, you are bound to see the *mallard* duck with her young chicks. In fact the Gearagh acts as a very important nursery for these birds, and is responsible for the large numbers found throughout the Lee valley. Dog owners please take note that mallard experience a very heavy moult after breeding and are not able to fly until the late summer. During this time they are extremely vulnerable to attack.

Usually moving fast, these summer visitors can be hard to distinguish in flight. However, their silhouettes are characteristic: top to bottom – swallow, martin, swift.

(5) On reaching a *sally*-smothered quarry island, the path proceeds, tunnel-like, through these water-loving trees. If you are observant you may be able to spot the ruined walls and fallen pillars of former buildings barely visible through the thicket of low branches and dense summer growth. These were once the homes of a close-knit community that lived around and on the ancient forest, in the townland of Annahala. Having survived the ravages of war, invasion and famine over several centuries these people were finally overtaken by modern

progress and had to sell their homes. Sadly, when the day came, many of the families gathered on the hill of Sleveen, and young and old stood weeping as they looked on their homes for the last time while the rising waters of the Lee hydroelectric scheme submerged them.

One old man refused to be driven from his ancestral home and became marooned on his now-island cottage, travelling in and out in the unique flat-bottomed boats that these people used to navigate the maze of channels in the swampy forest. Regrettably, he was drowned one night in a great flood as he returned to his lonesome hearth.

As you pass through the sally trees you may notice the water-filled old quarry on your left, behind the trees. Do not be tempted to venture any closer as it is over 100ft/30m deep, with sheer cliff sides. It never has any birds on it and thus is of little interest. So stick to the path.

Additionally, you may notice the characteristic straight line about 4ft/1.25m up on the trunks of the sally trees, very clearly delineated by the bottom line of *lichen* growth. This marks the winter water level when the reservoir is full. A sobering thought when you realise that they can fill it from empty to full in a matter of eight hours! Fortunately, the Electricity Supply Board, who now own the area, do make an attempt to keep the water levels low and the area accessible to the public during the summer months.

The trees themselves provide a welcome sanctuary for small songbirds in the middle of the reservoir, so keep an eye out for *long-tailed tits*, *finches* and *sparrows*, busily searching for insects amongst the purple *fumitory*, white *guelder* and pink *dog-rose* that grow through the branches.

Forming spectacular displays in summer, the purple loosestrife turns the sterile winter muds into gardens of purple haze.

(6) Just at the end of the quarry lake,

17

The spindle tree is not easily noticed in summer, but in autumn one is richly rewarded with its bright colours that light up the otherwise fading hedgerows.

before you leave the *sally* trees a small clearing opens up. STOP. You are now at the old quarry crossroads. This is very indistinct so watch carefully for the rather obscure path going off to your RIGHT. If you have come out of the trees completely you have missed the turn-off. The path follows the line of the old road that went west to Annahala. Walk along the road, which is covered in flowers during the summer and autumn. Look for the *purple loosestrife*, *marsh ragwort*, *sneezewort*, *mint* and *creeping jenny* that jostle with one another for space – they too are losing their natural habitats as the surrounding meadowlands are turned into sterile green deserts.

(7) Shortly, after about 30m, you come to a stile. Cross it, then keep going straight, pass through a gate (closing it behind you) and then a second gate a further 100m on. The latter exits onto a tarred road that immediately forks.

(8) At the fork, take the LEFT route, ignoring the apparently better track that swings right. Pass the well-kept farm on your left and follow the quiet country lane west. In autumn, keep an eye out for the edible *greengage* and *plum* amongst the hedgerow bushes, but avoid the poisonous, though beautiful, salmon-red fruits of the rarer *spindle tree* which is a native of the Alps and in Ireland is generally confined to the south-west.

(9) After 1.5km or so you will come to another Y-junction, just past the two cottages on your right. Go LEFT, following the road up, to

eventually pass the pitch-and-putt club on your left.

(10) Across from the pitch-and-putt club lies a fine stretch of bogland that turns white in summer with the many flower-heads of bog cotton. In late summer evenings, listen for the unique 'drumming' sound of the *snipe*, a sound it actually makes with its wings.

(11) The road eventually arrives at a very obvious T-junction. Go LEFT, to swing around the more marshy fens of the Gearagh. Here fine stands of the *greater reedmace* with their brown spike heads march across the swampy terrain to your left. This plant provides an excellent home for *waterhen* and *mallard* duck as it offers good cover as well as nesting sites, with ample food being found amongst the rich humus of the floating rafts of roots.

The greater reedmace is recognised by its tall stems on top of which sit the cigar-shaped seed-heads.

(12) After 0.5km or less, you will reach Dromkeen Cross, with its central grassy island. On your LEFT, there will be a small carpark. Enter into this and exit through the stile on the LEFT. Quite soon you will pick up the footpath again as it swings RIGHT onto the grass-covered old road lined with alder trees.

(13) As you walk along the path you pass the swampy tract again, on your left. In summer it is full of the colourful *damselflies* and *dragonflies*. These are easily distinguished from one another by the fact that *damselfly* always closes its wings at rest while the *dragonfly* keeps them spread open. Watch for the spectacular prussian-blue *banded agrion damselfly* that is extremely plentiful in June and July. Do not be tempted to enter the fen-like marsh where the *reedmace* form floating

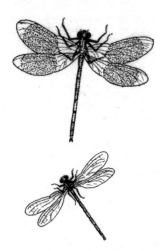

In the flower meadows you will spot the bright blue-green demoiselle damselfly (top) and the more numerous large red demoiselle (bottom).

Contrast the stronger-looking dragonfly (top) that keeps its wings open, with the more fragile damselfly (bottom) that folds its wings over its back.

rafts of vegetation with their spreading roots. These quiver and shake when stood upon, but can just as quickly open up to drop you into the dank bog-water holes beneath! Stick to the path. To the right the drier fields support good swards of the tall daffodil-like *yellow flag*, which flowers from May to July. Occasionally, you will come across a herd of cattle that are rather inquisitive and tend to follow you, but they are harmless.

(14) Soon you come to a concrete and wire-fenced stile. Pass through it and continue along the broken road that will lead you back to the quarry cross (6). Keep a look out across the water on your right, as it is here you are likely to see most of the many birds. In summer, hundreds of *mute swans* move into the reservoir to feed upon the lush plants that thrive in the muddy shallows, their white shapes contrasting sharply with the blackened oak stumps. From October onwards great flocks of winter migrants descend upon the reservoir. *Whooper swans, greylag geese, teal, mallard, wigeon, tufted* and *shoveler ducks, curlew, lapwing, golden plover* and *coot* all arrive in their thousands. Don't forget to look up, as it is in the sky that you are first likely to see the locust-like swarms of *golden plover* and *lapwing*.

(6) Pass STRAIGHT through the quarry cross again and out onto the causeway. As you wander back towards the gateway (1), keep an eye out for the beautifully coloured great crested grebe, which sometimes nests upon

isolated tree stumps. In August the *purple loosestrifes* and yellow *hawkweeds* line the old road. Please leave them there for the pleasure of others.

From autumn to the following spring large flocks of colourful lapwing line the shoreline. Their curious long thin head-crest makes them readily distinguishable.

# 2 – Ballyvourney

MUCH OF THE UNIQUE LANDSCAPE OF WEST CORK'S INTERIOR is typified by a complex web of heather-clad, rocky hills and hidden, deep valley folds that are straddled by an even more intricate mesh of lost and half-forgotten by-roads. Here a unique and priceless treasury of Irish heritage still survives, both in human terms as well as in a rich bounty of wildlife, the complex topography having dictated a slow pace of change for centuries.

The head of the picturesque river Sullane, that flows down from the Derrynasaggart Mountains, is one such spot. All around a patchwork of hedgerowed farms dresses the more fertile slopes, their lower boggy tracts and river gorges cloaked in woods of *silver birch*, *hazel* and *oak*. The picturesque farmsteads of stone, surrounded by their protective towering ash trees, spill out onto the meadows and laneways – hens and reeks of turf, haysheds bursting with the summer's reaping and haggards full of fattening calves. Each and every farming task in its slot, as much as the farming communities are themselves, with their strong sense of place, maintaining traditions that date far back into time. Irish is still the preferred tongue here in this beautiful *Gaeltacht* area of Coolea and Ballyvourney.

Traditions abound, full of history and pious enigma that may seem strange to the outsider, yet their constancy speaks for itself. The foundations of the civilization that first occupied the area lie scattered about the fields in monuments of stone, dating back thousands of years, their ways now lost to us. Later waves of people left more permanent legacies that are still as much a part of present culture as they were 1,300 years ago. This was the time of St Gobnait, the patron saint of the district, who founded a nunnery here in the seventh century. Sitting above the village of Ballyvourney are the remains of one of her many shrines – her church, sacred well and grave. Here 'rounds' are still performed in memory of the saint – prayers are said whilst walking around according to a strict rule or pattern. Many cures are said to have taken place here. Gobnait's feastday is celebrated on Whit Sunday and this is the only time the thirteenth-century oak figure of the saint is unveiled for the faithful. Many stories exist about the shrine, and it is up to oneself to decide on the authenticity of them, but no one can deny the power of faith and tradition.

## WALK DESCRIPTION

LOCATION: The walk begins in the village of Ballyvourney on the main Cork-Killarney road, 10ml/16km west of Macroom town or 18ml/24.5km east of Killarney. The start of the walk is located in the deciduous forest park of Coill Ghort na Tiobraide or St Gobnait's Wood. This is directly across the road from the Mills Inn tavern. Cross the stone bridge over the river Sullane at the junction, and enter the carpark immediately on your LEFT.

TERRAIN: A fine walk through the woods and along the quiet by-roads that snake around and about the undulating hills and valleys. It is ideal for all types, both young and old, following at first a simple path and later the narrow tarred roads that are practically free of all traffic.

LENGTH: 7.5ml/12km.

TIME: 3.5 hours.

FEATURES: Eighteenth-century beech woodland, St Gobnait's Shrine, ring fort, standing stones, picturesque farmsteads, wooded hedgerows, oak and hazel woods, landscape views of mountain, moor and wooded valley.

EQUIPMENT: Comfortable walking shoes with spare boots for an odd boggy part that can occur during wet weather.

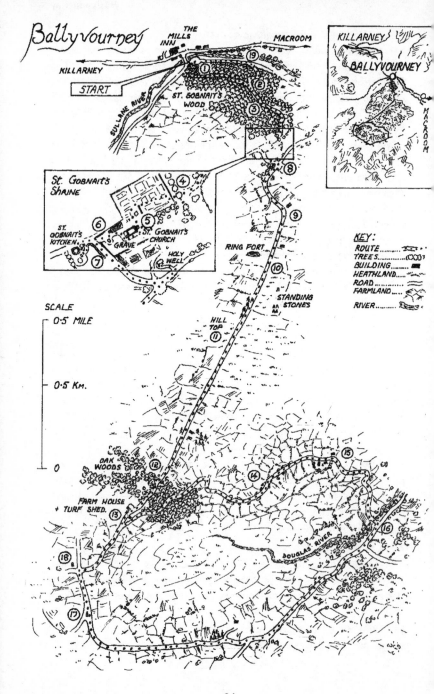

## WALK OUTLINE

(1) Go through the entrance at the carpark of Choill Ghort na Tiobraide, but instead of following the footpath straight ahead, look to your RIGHT. Take the stepped path on the side of the grassy embankment. This is where our walk begins – uphill through the woods. The pathway winds up through the fine old beech wood which was planted by the eighteenth-century settler family, the Colthursts. They were the landlords of the region, owning vast tracts of land over the surrounding mountains and moorlands. The romantic ruins that now enhance the gardens of the Mills Inn, visible through the trees and across the river behind you, are the remains of their former hunting lodge.

Here in the woodland, a good mix of native *oak*, *silver birch*, *holly* and *hazel*, has colonised the terrain. The trees are cloaked in rich growths of *moss*, thriving in the moist climate of Ireland's south-west. Across the woodland floor, tufts of the tall spike-like *hard fern* encircle the tree trunks, while drooping clumps of the rarer Lusitanian plant, *St Patrick's cabbage*, hang from the rocks. This is one of those plants unique to Ireland's south-west, not being found in either Britain or mainland Europe, which has prompted some people to suggest that it is a possible survivor from pre-Ice Age times and thus a 'dinosaur' plant of sorts.

(2) As the route levels out at the top of the wood you will eventually come to a fork in the path. Continue up to your RIGHT.

(3) Presently you will pass through a metal stile, after which you come to a more open clearing. Here the path becomes muddy and passes beside a sheep wire fence, on your left.

(4) Follow the path to its end where an iron stepped stile leads you over a wall into the graveyard. Follow the paths up to the top of the graveyard to arrive at the stone buildings and roofed church which you can see above.

(5) This is St Gobnait's Shrine. The old ruin on your left is the remains of her seventh-century church, now lost in a sea of headstones, monuments to those who in later times wished to be buried in this sacred spot. There is a more modern nineteenth-century church on your right. Please respect the sanctity of the shrine by remaining quiet, especially when people are praying and carrying out the rounds. Pass around by the LEFT-HAND SIDE of the ruined church and walk past its arched doorway to arrive at the front corner gable. Here a few stone

Many traditional farmhouses are surrounded by rich flower meadows.

steps on your right lead you into a small stone enclosure.

As you mount the steps look up at the gable wall to see a hole just above your head. Inside the hole and wedged tightly between the stones is St Gobnait's Bowl, a large round ball. This was said to have had magical powers in the hands of the saint and when thrown at pagan chieftains destroyed their fortresses. And after each throw the stone always returned to her hand. When she died, the bowl was preserved by her followers and handed down from one generation to the next, retaining the power to cure sick animals who were rubbed with it. The bowl was thus borrowed by the surrounding farmers in time of need and always returned when the curative properties had worked. However the bowl was eventually stolen by a miserly type who began to charge his neighbours for the benefit of its powers. But as soon as he received his first payment for the deed the bowl immediately flew out of his hand and returned to St Gobnait's Shrine, lodging steadfastly in the hole where it remains to this day! A cloth rubbed to it is said to have curative properties when later applied to sick animals.

(6) Coming back down the steps go RIGHT. Leaving the church behind you head towards the entrance gate situated in the north-west corner up to your RIGHT. Watch for the large mound on your left as you approach the gate. This is the grave of St Gobnait around which the rounds follow.

(7) Exit through the gate. You will be going LEFT and DOWNHILL along the tarred road. Directly on a height above you is the statue of St

Gobnait, made in 1950 by the well-known Cork sculptor Seamus Murphy, near St Gobnait's Well. It is here that the traditional rounds begin. Nearby also is a fine example of a circular neolithic house which would once have had a timber roof thatched with straw. It is known locally as St Gobnait's Kitchen, and the rounds move through it. You may wish to explore, and take a cool drink before heading on. Now go DOWNHILL along the tarred road.

(8) Follow the road down the hill, passing the farm buildings on your left. Soon you come to a junction with a stream flowing under the road. The route swings up to the RIGHT. However you may be interested to know that down the road to your left, about 150ft/50m, is another holy well which is said to bring about many cures. It is here that the round finishes, and if a cure is to happen then the person requesting it must empty the well! If fish appear at the bottom, a cure will be granted. Stories abound that lay claim to cures occurring, but just as many more about those who were disappointed.

(9) If you have visited the well, return to the junction at point (8). The road gradually rises up out of the wooded valley and leads towards the higher moors. In summer, the treeless hedgerows are full of the small, hardier *frothen* bushes, which produce tiny black edible berries. These jostle for space with the *heather* that spills out from the boggy heath. Streams pour down along the road-side margin, allowing the water-loving and heavily scented *meadow sweet* to grow in rich profusion from June to August. In open stretches of the grassy road margin the pink *heath spotted-orchid* may occur. It is sad to think that a lot of these once common plants are disappearing, mainly due to modern agricultural trends which are sterilising the entire landscape. Their last refuge is the roadside.

(10) As you approach the hilltop, watch for the earthen ring fort in a field on your right. Half-smothered in bracken and gorse it may be a bit hard to pick out from the many walls of the surrounding small meadows. Ring forts were built for the protection of homesteads from wild animals and this one was very probably lived in at the time of St Gobnait. Higher up and a little farther on, in the boggy field to the left of the road, are a number of standing stones – one pair and a group of four. The function of standing stones is more mysterious, no one knowing for sure if they had a religious purpose or were used purely to track seasons and time. Their original date, along with the ring fort, is still uncertain but may go as far back as 1000 BC. What they do show is that there was

The jay is an elusive bird usually seen only as it flies off out of sight.

a thriving community here, with little of their way of life now known to us other than their monuments, some of their customs and a later form of their language.

(11) On reaching the top of the hill, good views open up in front of you and to your right. These are the Derrynasaggart Mountains. A series of expansive uplands full of moorland wildlife, such as *grouse*, *woodcock*, *harriers* and *hares*. The characteristic heathland flowers grow in great profusion too, carpeting the bogs in sheets of colour during the spring and summer months. Look for the more common, blue-flowered *heath milkwort* from May to August or the yellow *bog asphodel* during July, August and September. Regrettably, in time, these too will disappear with all the other unique moorland flora beneath a suffocating canopy of sterile coniferous plantations. Already, these monotonous expanses of evergreen trees can be seen spreading across the lower mountain slopes, swallowing up many of the hard-won but now abandoned farms. It seems that soon there will be no place left for our wild partners as the human animal reaches up to rape even the mountain peaks themselves.

(12) Continue on DOWN the hill, passing some farmhouses on your left. Soon afterwards, in the valley bottom, some fine old oak woods come into view. These are a group of trees that have so far been spared the ravages of modern farming intensification. They offer the best use of this steep, rocky outcrop, providing shelter to livestock during intense heat, thus improving the quality of the holding, as well as offering sanctuary for predatory birds like *owls* that keep down pests such as *rats*. Watch for *squirrels*, *jays* and *kestrels* which still find safety in little pockets of undisturbed habitats like this. Edible nuts can be picked from the roadside – *hazels* in September.

(13) On passing through the wooded road you will soon come to some more farm buildings on your right. Just beyond these watch for an abandoned hayshed (illustrated on next page) behind which is a muddy by-road that doubles back up on your LEFT. Take this LEFT turn up and

through some charming *hazel* woods, keeping an eye out for *long-tailed tits*, *chaffinches* and *wrens* that find plenty to feed on in the undisturbed wild copses.

(14) The route now continues along some fine stretches of wooded farms and their accompanying romantic farmsteads. *Honeysuckle* scent fills the country lanes in June, its colourful flowers attracting the *meadow browns*, *peacocks* and *tortoise-shell* butterflies. Many native and well-known song birds can also be seen in the *hawthorn* hedgerows. *Blackbirds*, *robins*, *wrens*, *thrushes* and *tits* are especially plentiful, with their early-morning spring chorus being worth the rise in the month of April. Such out-of-the-way hedgerowed by-roads are still thankfully free of horrific and carcinogenic weedkillers, therefore allowing numerous wildflowers to grow. The hedgerows may appear to be drab and sombre places in winter, but the delight of the sudden symphony of wild blossoms that crowd the hedge bottom in spring and summer is an experience not easily forgotten. It is a memory that is etched deep into every child's mind, its sheer impact spurring their innocent imagination to pick the proverbial bunch of wild flowers for teacher or mum. In April and May the yellow *primroses*, purple *dog-violets* and white *stitchwort* festoon the overgrown stone walls. In July and August the purple *sheeps' bit* and tall *foxglove* are alive with the hum of bees and wasps. Come autumn, the lush bounty of

Turn to the left after this hayshed of turf. Many traditional farm buildings and implements are vanishing, thus it is delightful to find some still intact.

Watch along the road margins for the meadow browns feeding on the wild flowers.

*blackberry* fruits is the jam-maker's delight. The vast store of these clean, organic berries is still picked locally to make the homemade jams of the Coolea-based cottage industry, An Follain, which are sold in many food stores throughout the country.

(15) Continuing on along the country road some picturesque farmsteads are met. Around them stand their sheltering copse of *ash* and *pine* trees, which in early March will be a clattering din of squawking rooks. These large black birds, recognisable from other members of the crow family by their baggy trousers, return to the same rookery each year having spent the winter nights with thousand of others in their winter rookery several miles away in St Gobnait's Wood. If you take this walk in winter and are lucky enough to arrive back at the wood just as dusk descends, then you will be immediately struck by the thunderous clamour of the rooks as they arrive in mighty flocks to spend the night in the trees. Having travelled from all the surrounding countryside they arrive, regular as clockwork, to squawk and scream before settling down for the night. A common enough phenomenon, but rarely seen because of their late arrival and the winter weather that keeps one by the fireside. However it is an experience well worth the effort.

(16) Eventually, the road meanders down the hillside towards a wooded

The dog-violet is a common plant of the less overgrown hedgerows.

valley, to arrive at a T-junction. The small river Douglas passes under the bridge, pouring down from the wooded gorge just above. Go RIGHT, following this slightly busier road for 1.25ml/2km. Ignore the turn-off to the left just ahead, as well as the next two left turns and right one farther on. The road meanders around wooded hills to eventually open out into more open farmland. These fields are not without their attendant wild birds though. From October to the following March, the rich bounty of *hawthorn* and *holly* berries provides winter feeding for many flocks of native species.

(17) After 1.25ml/2km a forked road is reached amidst open countryside. This fork has a grassy island in the middle. Go to the RIGHT which will bring you to a four-crossroad junction just a little further on.

(18) At the crossroads take the small side-road up to the RIGHT. This returns you to another quiet country by-road that leads back up the hill. About 0.25ml/0.4km later you arrive back at point (13) where you turned up the muddy laneway after the farmhouse and picturesque hayshed of turf that is now on your right. At this farmhouse go STRAIGHT on, retracing your footsteps back up the hill and to St Gobnait's Shrine.

(5) At the shrine go back down through the graveyard, over the stepped iron stile and into the wood again. Follow the path down through the trees until you come to a fork (2). Go to the RIGHT, taking the steep descent downhill until a grassy forest track is met.

(19) On reaching the forest track, go to the LEFT which brings you straight back to the carpark (1).

# 3 – Gougane Barra

SURROUNDED BY THE TOWERING CLIFFS of heather-clad peaks and endless seas of upland heath, the sixth-century hermitage of St. Finbarr sits on a small island in a mountain-locked tarn. This was all the sanctuary he needed. At his back and to the west stretched the extensive and untamed uplands of the Cork and Kerry Mountains; to the east the once deeply-forested, glaciated valley of the River Lee. Now, winding its way out of Gougane Barra's coomb, the Lee passes through a patchwork quilt of hedgerowed farms, oak-hazel woods and quiet country lanes, while the raw wilderness of the Shehy mountains at its source has changed little over the centuries.

This is an area rich in both wildlife and history, with many of the unusual species of the south-west readily observed here. Its rare *Lusitanian* flora and fauna are one such group, thriving in the many sheltered valleys carved out of the old red sandstone rocks. It is believed that they are an ancient group of species that somehow survived the Ice Age and really belong to another time. They are most certainly a strange collection, not found elsewhere other than in a small corner of northern Portugal. Their origin remains a total mystery to us.

Within Gougane, many paths meander about the lower slopes, amongst rock-strewn streams and coniferous woods. Others lead to the higher ground where waves of *heather, bog myrtle* and *frothen* sweep sea-like across the untouched moorlands. Drifting away endlessly into the vastness of distant mountain peaks stand ancient folds of boney rock, skeletons of another time, pushed up in mighty earth upheavals before the dawn of life. Now their remoteness and wild ruggedness offer a last refuge to the rare and strange, as well as many more common members of our native wildlife heritage.

## WALK DESCRIPTION

LOCATION: 42mls/67km west of Cork city on the Macroom-Bantry road. Watch for the well-signposted turn off, 4.5mls/7km west of the village of Ballingeary.

TERRAIN: A fairly strenuous uphill walk to a high mountain ridge of heath and rock, that has no well-defined path, and from which one can descend at fixed points only. Like any mountain area, it is prone to mist during inclement weather, and can be fairly wet and boggy. Therefore one needs to be sensible, exercise caution and be suitably equipped. It is not advisable to enter the high mountains alone.

LENGTH: 6mls/10km

TIME: 4 hours

FEATURES: St. Finbarr's island hermitage; medieval pilgrimage path and mountain stairs; source of the river Lee; good tracts of wilderness with heathland flora and fauna; the Kerry spotted slug; excellent views towards Bantry Bay; Ice Age features.

EQUIPMENT: Water-resistant mountain boots with good grip; a light, wind and water-resistant jacket; knapsack to carry a warm jumper, some food and liquid; OS map, Discovery series no. 85.

## WALK OUTLINE

(1) Arriving at Gougane Barra, easy parking is available by the hotel or near the island church, which marks the site of St. Finbarr's hermitage. Follow the lake-side road towards the forest park.

Here, during the sixth century, St. Finbarr lived a life of isolation and prayer. Access to the spot would have been extremely difficult at this time, since the entire area was cloaked in aboriginal oak forest, full of *wolf* and *boar*. Still, if the need arose, he had his escape route ready. Far

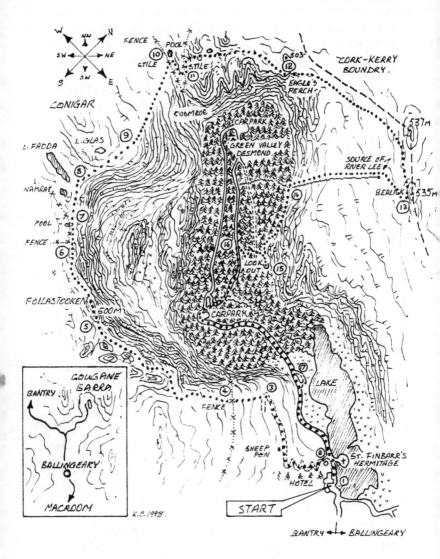

Gougane Barra

34

from being cornered within a coomb of precipitous cliffs, a well-concealed, man-made staircase, built into the side of the cliff at the back of the valley, led quickly to freedom. Here one can still become beautifully lost, in the many hidden valleys of the Cork and Kerry Mountains. The island, now connected to the mainland by a more modern causeway, is still a very important Catholic pilgrimage site for the people of Cork, St. Finbarr having been the first bishop of Cork city. A carved head of the saint is visible over the doorway of the more modern church, which is based on the design of St. Cormac's chapel on the Rock of Cashel. Also, a seventeenth-century reconstruction of the hermit's cells can be seen at the rear of the island, within which a number of holy rounds are performed before the carved Stations of the Cross. It can be quite busy on Sundays, and you may prefer to explore when you come back later in the evening after the walk, even though early morning is best.

(2) Leaving the hermitage behind you on your right, continue to walk for a short distance STRAIGHT along the lakeside road. Then, after a few metres, take the laneway up to your LEFT, just beside the unusual, thatched public toilets. Pass through the gate, reclosing it after you, and follow the track up the hill. As the back of the hotel comes into view the track doubles back up the hill. Follow it as it zigzags upwards, opening and reclosing the second gate. After a concrete sheep-pen, the track runs out onto the open heath, with the coniferous-covered coomb in front of you.

(3) Follow the track as it zigzags up the hill, finally ending near the edge of the conifer plantation. Here, cross the wire fence by using the metal stile to the LEFT of an iron gate and continue to follow the rising ground.

A mixture of *Sitka spruce, Douglas fir, pine* and *larch* now cover the floor of 'deep-vallied Desmond'. It is now very different in appearance from the time it was so romantically described by the seventeenth-century Cork poet JJ Callanan, in his well-known poem on Gougane:

*There is a green island in lone Gougane Barra,*
*Where Allua of song rushes forth as an arrow,*
*In deep-vallied Desmond – a thousand wild fountains*
*Come down to that lake from their home in the mountains.*
*There grows the wild ash, and a time-stricken willow*
*Looks chidingly down on the mirth of the billow.*

(4) Having crossed the fence at the stile continue UP through the rockier terrain, heading for the highest point of Foilastookeen, at 500m. Stay close to, but back from, the rising cliffs that are on your right.

The coomb is a fine example of glacial action. Still fresh and impressive-looking, it was carved out of the surrounding mountains by Ireland's last glaciation, the Cork-Kerry ice sheet, which finally ended about 10,000 years ago.

About the wetter areas grow numerous specimens of that most beautiful of all Irish wildflowers, the *greater butterwort (Pinguicula grandifolia)*. It is also one of the most unusual ones. Not found on mainland Europe, it is believed to be a hangover from before the Ice Age. A member of the rare *Lusitanian* group, this area is one of its main headquarters on the planet (don't even think of picking it!). Its basal rosette of sticky, green leaves traps the tiny insects of the bogs and absorbs their protein-rich nutrients into its tissues. This is to extract the valuable nitrogen it needs for growth, a mineral practically absent in the peaty soil. So it would be wrong to describe them as flesh eaters.

Butterwort – its beauty belies its function. Not able to obtain the necessary nitrogen from the boggy soil, it traps insects in its sticky leaves and absorbs the necessary nutrients.

(5) On reaching the pinnacle of Foilastookeen, the ascent continues to the next highest point and then begins to swing westwards, to the right.

If you are not used to such steep ascents, remember to rest for a minute or so as often as you require. This helps one to catch ones breath and gradually acclimatise. With the rising ground, the distant mountains of neighbouring Kerry start to come into view on your right. These are the Reeks. On a clear day, the apex of Carrauntouhill, Ireland's highest peak at 3414ft/1035m, should be discernible.

(6) Presently, a sheep wire fence comes up from the left and then

continues westwards, up and along the ridge top. Follow it to the highest point ahead. Southwards the land falls away through much heathland, down to numerous hedgerowed farms. Further to the south-west, Bantry Bay and Whiddy Island make their appearance. Beyond these lies the Dunmanus peninsula and, beyond that again, the peaks of Mizen Head poking out into the Atlantic Ocean.

Looking straight across to the other side of the valley, you should be able to discern the rounded top of Bealick. It is from here that you will descend down to the tree line, following the course of the emerging river Lee.

(7) Up here the path is well worn and begins to drop down again. Follow it until you arrive at a small pool, with a stone-slabbed footbridge. Leaving the fence, you continue UP and STRAIGHT on until the second of the next two adjoining lakes are visible on your left.

As you walk, keep an eye open for the wild *red deer* that migrate to these hills from nearby Killarney. If you are very patient, and very lucky, you might also see *kestrels, sparrow hawks* and *grouse*.

(8) On passing the second and larger lake, Lough Fada, start to turn to the RIGHT and work your way up to the front spur of Conigar, circling around the back of the coomb. If you stay up high and well back from the cliffed edge you should shortly pass by the small Lough Glas. Here a timber stile will lead you over the sheep wire fence. Keep the fence on

The red grouse is strictly a bird of the heather-clad moors, feeding on young
heather shoots. Sadly, because of burning, sheep grazing and coniferous
afforestation, their numbers are declining.

your right as you descend the slope.

From here there are fine views eastwards, back down the Lee valley. By the first body of water sits the Irish-speaking hamlet of Ballingeary. Further east again, the second body of water brings us to the artists' retreat of Inchigeelagh. Lastly, if there is no haze, the third body of water indicates the wildlife haven of the Gearagh near Macroom, my home town.

(9) From Lough Glas, the open expanse of purple moor grass runs in a billowing sward down to the back of 'Coomroe' and a sheep wire fence. Descend diagonally and locate a foot stile in the fence. This will be near the small pool that you can see below.

Looking westwards – to your left – there are fine views across the Borlin Valley and up to the peaks of Knockboy and the unusual hanging lake, Lough Nambrackderg ('lake of the red trout'). After rain, a delightful waterfall slides tinsel-like down its precipitous rear wall.

(10) On reaching the fence, cross it using the stile and then go diagonally away over to the RIGHT, to reach another fence with its well-hidden stile, behind a large boulder.

(11) Having crossed the second fence, go immediately to the LEFT, going up and around the rock escarpment in order to avoid the deep clefts in the rocks that will present themselves ahead (check the map).

Having left the rocks behind, the heath opens up again and it is a reasonably easy trek across to the other side of the coomb, to a point where I love to sit, relax and daydream, just in front of the 503m mark. Watch for the *skylarks* that regularly move out from underfoot to break the empty silence, their gentle chorus echoing on the wind as they flutter above your head.

(12) Before pushing on I always take time out at this point. Here a grassy knoll hangs atop the cliffs, just above the carpark and what I selfishly like to call my 'eagle's perch'. It is on this spot that I have sat a thousand times since childhood, sorting out life's problems and making career decisions. Sitting here hawk-like above the world, one gets a great sense of control over the turmoil of daily life that goes on below, and I always come home feeling renewed.

When you feel rested, it is best to swing in a wide arc out and up to your RIGHT, making for the peak of Bealick at 535m (not 537m). It is best to stay up high, following the line of the Cork-Kerry border indicated on the map.

(13) A heap of stones marks the top of Bealick. From here descend south-westwards, to the RIGHT, locating the emerging river Lee, which will be below and to the right again. Then follow it down to a footpath just above the tree line. Don't be tempted to go straight down, as the terrain contains extremely wet and overgrown quagmires.

Northwards from Bealick, fine views extend over the expansive tracts of moorland that epitomise the Derrynasaggart mountains. Away in the distance you should be able to recognise the conspicuous breasts of 'The Paps', home of our ancient Celtic goddess, Dana (see *Kerry Walks*). Straight out to the west, in a line with the mountains you are now on, are the Caha peaks that form the Bere peninsula. These plummet into the sea at Allihes.

If you are lucky enough to locate the river Lee's source, it is interesting to see its simple beginnings. Bubbling up in a small pool from the turf and surrounded by green clumps of *sphagnum moss*, it rises mysteriously out of some subterranean stream deep within the mountains.

(14) Having arrived at the forest footpath, turn to the LEFT and follow it down, eventually arriving into the woods. Further down you will have to detour slightly to the LEFT to arrive at the 'look-out' point. This is an ancient footpath that led pilgrims from the western regions, such as Kilgarvin and Kenmare, down into the pilgrimage site of Gougane Barra.

On entering the woods, *larch* trees tower overhead. The only deciduous conifers in Ireland, they shed their needles in autumn with an impressive splash of yellows and golden-browns. The resulting light that gets in has allowed many of our displaced native plants to recolonise this part of the woods. Plenty of *holly* and the more characteristic *mountain ash* grow here, while beneath them can be found the delicate, white-flowered *wood sorrel* of spring.

It is also in places like this that you may encounter the well known, but rarely seen, *Kerry spotted slug*. This is another of the unique *Lusitanian* species, recognisable by its creamy-white spots and its habit of curling up

The Kerry spotted slug reaches the eastern edge of its range here in the mist-shrouded hills of West Cork.

like a hedgehog when touched. It is very likely that this is a hangover species from before the Ice Age, two million years ago, when it inhabited a very different world. If you find it, please treat it with the respect such a rare creature deserves.

(15) At the 'look out' you can see back down to the lake from the timber fence. If you are standing at the left-hand corner of the 'look out', lean out a bit further and you will see the ancient stairs coming up through the rocks below you. This is the old path used by pilgrims in centuries gone by, as they came from the mountain valleys beyond to worship at Gougane. Remarkably, it descends all the way down the side of the valley and must also have been an excellent escape route during times of trouble, to get out of this otherwise imprisoning coomb. It is now very dilapidated, with some parts vanishing over sheer cliffs. It would not therefore be advisable to attempt descending it, with most of it lost in high grass and ferns.

From the 'look out', retrace your steps BACK along the path for about thirty metres and follow it downwards. After a while it crosses a forest track, but ignore this and follow the steep footpath down to the tarred road.

(16) On reaching the road, go to the LEFT and follow it up by the carpark and toilets. Continue to follow the road OUT of the park and eventually

along by the lake back to the island hermitage. As you walk along the road you may notice how the dark shade caused by the imported coniferous trees allows very little life to exist upon the woodland floor, other than moss and fern. It is also in rocky places like this that you are likely to spot the Kerry spotted slug, mentioned above.

Dependent on small meadows for its continued survival, the yellow bartsia can survive only in the less profitable small holdings amongst the rocky hills.

(17) Fine views of the lake and its picturesque island church accompany you back to the carpark. Watch the waters for the rare alpine *water lobelia* during the summer months, its reddish stems projecting out of the shallows and bearing delicate pink-white flowers. A plant that is more accustomed to alpine conditions, it has a very restricted distribution in

Ireland, being confined to the extreme west. Its presence indicates that the water is slightly acidic. In the smaller meadows another rare plant can be found growing. This is the *yellow bartsia*, which has its headquarters in the south-west. It persists here, along with many more common meadow flowers, because of the lack of sterilisation of the fields by intensive farming.

(1) Refreshments may be had at the hotel (closed in winter), or you may prefer to relax amongst the trees and ruins of the hermitage. Opposite the island entrance, within the arched tomb, is the grave of Rev. Denis O'Mahony. He was responsible for the preservation of the hermitage, building the stone courtyard and cells towards the end of the sixteenth century. In fact, he spent the last days of his life living in them. Behind his tomb is a small graveyard, the last resting place of 'The Tailor and Ansty', local characters made famous in the book of the same name by Eric Cross. This book vividly describes the way of life that existed here during the earlier part of the century. Amazingly enough, the church banned the book when it was published, the old tailor being forced to his knees and made to burn the book in the fire. Some may say that 'good old innocent Ireland is dead and gone', but it is great to see the rebirth of our rich and ancient heritage after centuries of endemic religious and social repression. Long live the bard and the written word. And long live the rich memories of 'The Tailor and Ansty'.

The clapper bridge was a common sight in the early part of this century. However, many have disappeared through disuse and others have been bulldozed away.

# 4 – Coolkelure

THERE ARE NUMEROUS FORGOTTEN CORNERS hidden in the inner folds of West Cork. Many fertile little hamlets nestle in the winding and crooked valleys enclosed by rough mountainous terrain. These old farms weave up the rocky slopes, giving way to woods of silver birch and oak and finally to boggy heath. Mountain streams carve their way down through tilted meadows, at times opening out into silent pools and reed-locked lakes. Thus, in one localised area we get a wide diversity of habitats ranging from mountain and moor, through hedgerowed meadow and woodland, to river and lake – a characteristic variety that is unique to the more remote regions of West Cork. This is of major significance to the wildlife of the territory, so that a diverse range of species can exist, each surviving within its own particular niche. Furthermore, these areas act as significant nature banks that help many species escape the threat of extinction when the countryside faces the onslaught of intensive agriculture, with its farming techniques that demand the removal of all unprofitable regions. And so we get the total destruction of hedgerows and woods, the draining of bogs and marshes and the canalisation of streams and rivers – a landscape where nothing is allowed to exist other than chemicalised cows and imported strains of grass. This impoverishment becomes much more obvious when you compare an area of West Cork, like the Shehy Mountains north of Dunmanway, to the extensive and monotonous lowlands of Ireland's central plain or the sterile factory farms in other parts of Cork. In these nether regions the pressure of modern progress has wiped the last vestiges of wilderness from the land, leaving it devoid of most of its natural wildlife. It is essential to protect those areas still relatively intact.

## WALK DESCRIPTION

LOCATION: Within the small valley of Coolkelure beneath the summit of Nowen Hill, lost in the Shehy Mountains between Bantry and Dunmanway. The start of the walk is 19ml/30km from Bantry or 9ml/14.5km from Dunmanway at the forest park of Cullenagh Lake. This is not well signposted but if you travel the back road from Dunmanway to Bantry, take the right turn-off 6.5ml/10.5km beyond Dunmanway, which has a signpost for Inchigeelagh (14.5ml), ignoring the sign to your right for Coolkelure at the Y-junction just beyond the town. Then go left at the first Y-junction met, with another sign for Inchigeelagh (12.5ml). Soon after, watch for the signposted entrance to the coniferous forest park on your left.

TERRAIN: A gentle walk through the many backroads that encircle the valley. Ideal for anyone who likes a trouble-free, casual walk – with their hands in their pockets! (But a few cars will be met.)

LENGTH: 5.5ml/9km.

TIME: 2.5 hours.

FEATURES: Cullenagh Lake and Forest Park, Nowen Hill with the source of the river Bandon, deciduous and coniferous wooded roadways, views of the abandoned Coolkelure demesne amidst the mountainous heathlands, St Edmund's Church.

EQUIPMENT: comfortable walking shoes; wellingtons to cross a small stream.

## WALK OUTLINE

(1) Arriving at the forest carpark, you are looking down on the picturesque waters of Cullenagh Lake. Surrounded by newly planted conifers, the lake nestles beneath the tall peak of Nowen Hill, whose upper slopes are still home to some of the original oak woods that

44

formerly cloaked the valley. Straight in front of you and across the lake you should be able to see the rising river Bandon cascading down from its mountain source, flowing through acid peatlands and rocky ravines before entering the woods and finally spilling into the lake. Mats of *lilies* grow about the open water in summer, the lake margin becoming fringed with taller *reed*, which provide suitable cover and feeding areas for newly fledged *waterhens* and *mallard duck*. It is not uncommon to see a *raven* pair spiralling above, as they scour the broad tracts of boggy heath beneath, for carrion and small rodents. Ravens pair for life and start breeding as early as February, making their nest in the higher, cliffed ledges of the hills.

(2) Exit from the carpark, back out to the road, and go RIGHT. The road descends downhill, passing through some coniferous woods. Even though these trees are rather sterile, a number of birds have managed to adapt to them, such as the *cross-billed finches,* invaders from the Continent, who crack the seed cones open with their tough bills. Additionally, they also offer shelter to the tiny *goldcrest*, Europe's smallest bird, which is only 3.5in/9cm long. This bird can be hard to spot as it dodges about the higher branches in search of insects, but it is instantly recognisable by its striped golden crown.

Smaller than the wren, the goldcrest is only 9cm from beak to tail.

(3) Passing down the hill, a metal barrier indicates the entrance to another coniferous plantation on the LEFT. This has been part clear-felled and replanted as of 2004. Turn into the forest along the open track and follow it through the trees, keeping an eye out for the many *finches* and *tits* that scramble about the upper branches. The trail through the wood can at first appear monotonous, but being free of traffic and interference it does allow the wildlife to move more freely about, using the trees as corridors to travel from one area of wilderness to another. So it is not uncommon to surprise a *fox* or *badger* as it crosses your path. Small rodents can also survive in young, immature

woods, and these will draw down the *sparrow hawk* and *owl* who hunt along these empty tracks. However, very few animals use or depend upon these evergreen trees as breeding sites, preferring overgrown wild patches that give greater protection and a wider selection of food.

(4) Moving on through the wood, a stream crosses the track. There are some crude stepping stones, but in rainy weather you will need wellington boots to cross.

(5) Soon afterwards you arrive at a T-junction. Go RIGHT, the track rising gradually up through the trees to a Y-junction. Go LEFT, and follow the track up and out onto a tarred road. This area has also been clear-felled as of 2004, but a rough track leads up to another metal barrier and the tarred road.

(6) On reaching the road, go to your LEFT. Coming out of the woods, the old demesne of Coolkelure comes into view. Now being actively run as a modern farm, the remains of the nineteenth-century estate are quite obvious in the layout of the land. On your left you pass the imposing private residence that was once the dairy farm to the old demesne. Above it, on your right, is the dairy wood, now another plantation of *coniferous trees*. This was one of the numerous copses planted by the landlords as game coverts for their hunting forays in the last century. Most of these were originally *oak* and *beech* woods, but these were cut down during the Second World War and later planted with the quick-growing conifers. However, many large single trees remain to line the hedgerows and boundary fences or mark the site of former ornamental gardens.

(7). Shortly after the dairy farm you come to a junction at a bend, with a road going to your right. Take this RIGHT turn and continue along the road. In summer, from June to August, the low stone walls are festooned with the white flowers of *St Patrick's cabbage*, a plant that is unique to West Cork, where it grows in great profusion in the moist and sheltered valleys. It is a member of the rare Lusitanian group of plants native to West Cork and Kerry. Eventually the route passes by a farmhouse and goes through a short, wooded stretch of road. Ultimately the hedgerow on the left opens up, and fine views are revealed across the valley on your left, towards the rocky heathlands that encircled the estate. The wider open meadows are the hunting ground of the white *barn owl*, whom you will see emerging only at dusk, using the surrounding woods as lookout points to scan the fields for rats and mice. This area is now being actively quarried for its rich deposits of sand.

(8) Continuing on along the narrow roadway a T-junction is eventually met. Go LEFT, taking the road down through Derryduff wood, where the overgrown hedgerows of *rhododendron* merge with the adjacent trees. Here some felling of trees is taking place, which results in one of the more unfortunate side-effects of these plantations – as soon as a number of species colonise them and build up a viable population, they are immediately decimated by the removal of all the trees when they reach maturity.

(9) Soon another road forks off to the left, opposite the entrance to the coniferous plantation on the right. Ignore these and keep going STRAIGHT.

(10) The road falls gently downward, passing the private entrance to the old demesne mansion on your left,

The circular rosettes of shiny leathery leaves of the St Patrick's cabbage persist throughout the year, sending up the tall flower spikes in June.

Coolkelure House (not open to the public). Still in perfect condition, it sits snugly within its surrounding cloak of trees. It is a fine late-Victorian house of stone, with interesting gables of timber open-work in the Swiss style. The large timber door is decorated with bolts and hinges that give it a castle-like effect. The estate was planned out by the Shuldham family in the 1800s and later passed by inheritance to the fourth Earl of Bandon, through his wife Georgina, one of the Frekes of Castle Freke. The Earl also owned estates in Bandon and Macroom. All of these have since been decimated, their original presence remaining as mere shadows on a changed landscape. Passing on down the road, the walls become much larger and carry relict plants from the former ornamental gardens, such as *rhododendron*, *laurel* and other exotics. Peering through the hedge on your left, you can see the towering palms that mark the site of the landscaped grounds which surrounded the house.

(11) Presently, a Y-junction is reached with a small island in the middle of the cross, which has a young evergreen tree growing on it. Take the LEFT fork. At the junction and on your left-hand side is the former main

entrance to Coolkelure House, with its beautiful gate lodge still intact. The character of the lodge is quite impressive and seems to be out of place in this wild, mountainous countryside. Richly adorned with gargoyles and crests, it far exceeds the main residence itself for effect and gives the impression that it leads to some mysterious chateau, hidden high up in the forested mountains, like some Transylvanian castle in the remote regions of Romania. The lodge is now a private residence, with the old avenue itself, although still overshadowed by its original ornamental trees, leading to a sandpit.

(12) A short distance beyond the junction, the road passes over the small Garrown river to arrive at the entrance of St Edmund's church on your left. Set romantically amongst the trees the picturesque building has some interesting carved heads around its doorway. One headstone at the back of the church has the following inscription on it: 'John Hopkins, servant to Colonel Shuldham and Countess of Bandon'. This is the only written evidence visible here to tell of the presence of the former lords in the valley.

(13) Exiting from the church, go LEFT and continue up the hill, to the next junction. Just beyond the church and on your right, is the old, abandoned schoolhouse, hidden by a high and overgrown hedge. This

Quietly hidden amongst the trees, the picturesque limestone
building, St Edmund's Church, imparts a peace and
stillness to its surroundings.

was also built by the Shuldhams and here many of the children of the estate workers were educated. As you continue up the road, the reed-fringed waters of Coolkelure Lake come into view on your left. Now returned to the wilderness, it once was girdled by oak-canopied paths.

(14) Arriving at the Y-junction on top of the hill go LEFT. The route meanders through some hilly meadows, bordered by hedges of *hawthorn*. These bushes are a blaze of white flowers in early May, criss-crossing the landscape in ribbon-like strands. They

The fieldfares travel in flocks about the fields, feeding greedily on the bumper crops of berries that still survive in the remoter regions of the south-west.

provide a valuable supply of nectar to the first emerging insects when very few of the other summer flowers have blossomed. Then in winter these hedges are a wash of blood-red colour, their branches weighed down with the bumper crops of red-berried seeds or *haws*. These are eagerly sought out by *thrushes* and *blackbirds* when winter frosts harden the ground. Furthermore they provide a rich diet for the thousands of *redwings* and *fieldfares* that invade the fields in late autumn, birds that have migrated down from the colder climate of northern Scandinavia and Russia to spend the winter in Ireland.

(15) Following the road upwards, and over the hill, wide tracts of bog and mountain are visible to your right and in front of you. Across the valley, on your right, is the deciduous wood of Dreenwanish, an older remnant of the original woods, full of *silver birch* and *holly*. It is in pockets of wilderness like this that a greater diversity of species is found, deciduous woods providing a much larger range of habitats for our native species. And so we get animals like the *red squirrel, stoat* and *hedgehog*, as well as birds of prey such as the *merlin* and *sparrowhawk*.

(16) Continuing on down the hill the road forks, just beyond some

houses. Go LEFT.

(17) At the bottom of the hill, is a T-junction. Go LEFT, and follow the road back towards Nowen Hill, which should be visible in front of you. On the roadside, the hedges come alive with the chorus of song birds in early spring, each bird staking out its territory in rich dialogue in order to guarantee ample supplies of food for its intended fledgelings. In such pockets of wilderness that harmonise well with the surrounding farmland, you can check the state of health of the habitat, not by trying to find unusual species on their own, but by counting the number of different species you encounter. If you can count a dozen species, then all is fairly well.

(1) A little further on another Y-fork is met. Go LEFT. This brings you back to the forest park of Cullenagh Lake and the carpark.

(18) Within the carpark, a stepped path leads down to the shoreline. No nicer spot to picnic and finish the day.

All around the shoreline of Cullenagh Lake the four-spotted dragonfly can be seen as it rests on the lakeside vegetation.

# 5 – Castlefreke

THE COASTLINE OF WEST CORK is one of immense variety. Not alone does it offer wild mountain landscape, rich forested bays and miles of precipitous cliffs, but it is also encircled with extensive stretches of sandy beaches and dunes. In the region around Rosscarbery, the high rocky hills of the more western peninsulas lose their impact and the landscape becomes marked by long strips of golden sand. Here is an excellent place to experience the might of the Atlantic ocean as it crashes onto the sandy shore. Behind, the dunes barricade the land from the sea, growing during the tranquil summer weather and eroding during the wild winter gales. Dunes are unstable and harsh environments that allow only a very specific community to live on them. Any that can survive the excessive amounts of salt will readily thrive, but in response they are confined to this type of habitat only. Thus in summer the dunes are full of individual types of plant that are unusual and striking in appearance.

Winter has more to offer in the diversity of birds that will be encountered in these unique habitats. The coastline environment, though violent at its most extreme, has been the most consistent of habitats throughout time. This has allowed many types of plant and animal to evolve in union with its characteristics, especially the multitude of birdlife that crowds the coastal estuaries in winter, having migrated from the colder, northern regions around Iceland and Scandinavia.

Unfortunately, these same regions have become magnetic poles for humans who crowd the beaches in fine weather. To many, dunes are seen as sterile, wasteful places and thus open to all forms of exploitation. And so we get the spread of grotesque holiday homes, hotels and shanty shacks with their 'commanding views of the sea'. Then there is the inevitable need for trendy golfcourses across the remainder of the dunes – selfishness at its most blatant, as it destroys the fragile ecosystems of many rare life forms and shuts off the coastal environs to the greater public. Hopefully in time a more educated and respecting public will see the sense in protecting these rare ecosystems for the pleasure of all and of their wildlife occupants.

## WALK DESCRIPTION

LOCATION: 3ml/5km from Rosscarbery, or 7ml/11km from Clonakilty. The walk begins at the carpark of the Long Strand, 0.5ml/0.8km beyond the badly developed Ownahincha beach area. Travel from Rosscarbery, on the Rosscarbery-Clonakilty road for 1ml/1.6km. Take the well-signposted RIGHT turn off for Ownahincha beach. Pass the holiday homes, caravans and hotels that look onto the first beach, and proceed along the coast road to the undefiled Long Strand. This is hidden by extensive stretches of sand dunes and has a carpark on the opposite left-hand side of the road.

TERRAIN: An excellent walk along fine stretches of beach and dunes, then through the many laneways about the old demesne of Castle Freke. This is a circular walk that is completely off the roadways and it is suitable for all. As of 1998 much of the coniferous woodland has been harvested and the paths have become extremely muddy, especially after rain. Thus wellingtons are necessary.

FEATURES: Wave-washed beach; extensive dunes; reed-fringed lake; Castle Freke demesne and coniferous woods; oak and beech woods; the ruins of Castle Freke mansion, Rathbarry church and Rathbarry castle. There is a short OPTION available at the end of the walk to see the carved celtic cross that was erected to the ninth Baron Carbery.

LENGTH: 5.5ml/9km. The OPTION is 1ml/1.6km extra.

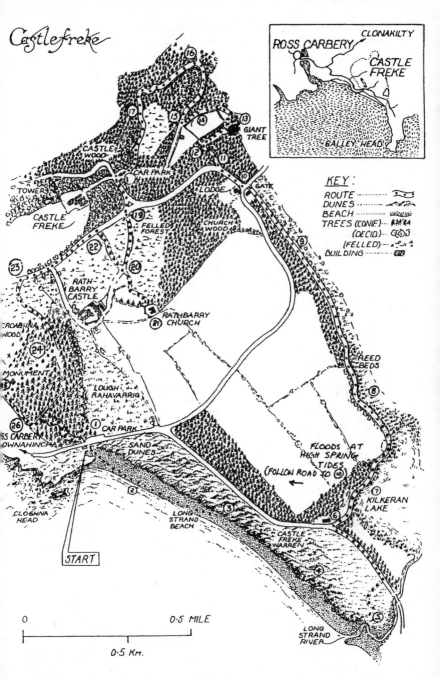

Castlefreke

CLONAKILTY

ROSS CARBERY

CASTLE FREKE

GALLEY HEAD

16

7   15   14   13
              GIANT
              TREE

CASTLE
WOOD

12   11

10

CAR PARK
              LODGE   GATE
TOWERS

CASTLE
FREKE

19

FELLED
FOREST

CHURCH
WOOD

22

KEY:
ROUTE
DUNES
BEACH
TREES (CONIF)
       (DECID)
       (FELLED)
BUILDING

23

20

9

RATH
BARRY
CASTLE

RATHBARRY
CHURCH
21

CROAGHNA
WOOD

24

REED
BEDS

MONUMENT

8

LOUGH
RAHAVARRIG

26

CAR PARK

RS CARBERY
OWNAHINCHA

SAND
DUNES

FLOODS AT
HIGH SPRING
TIDES
(FOLLOW ROAD TO 10)

2

7
KILKERAN
LAKE

CLOGHNA
HEAD

3

LONG
STRAND
BEACH

6

CASTLE
FREKE
WARREN

START

4

0        0.5 MILE

0.5 KM.

LONG
STRAND
RIVER

5

53

**TIME**: 3 hours. The OPTION takes 0.5 hours extra.

**EQUIPMENT**: Comfortable walking boots, but wellingtons are necessary for the now very muddy paths through the coniferous woods.

## WALK OUTLINE

(1) Go directly onto the beach by the open clearing in the dunes. This is near a small building, across the road from the *coniferous trees* and the carpark. Once on the beach go to the LEFT, following the long stretch of sand that disappears into the distance. On your right, before you begin to walk the beach is Cloghna Head, a high-cliffed promontory, about which fly many *fulmars*. These birds are similar in appearance to gulls, but are far more interesting. They spend much of their time on the open sea, only returning to land in late autumn and staying until the following breeding season. Fulmars are excellent fliers, negotiating in and out about the cliffs as they take advantage of the rising air currents. They are relative newcomers to the area, and were originally confined to the island of St Kilda off the coast of Scotland, just over one hundred years ago. But they have since spread right around the Irish coastline, having found some new niche for themselves in the food chains of the sea.

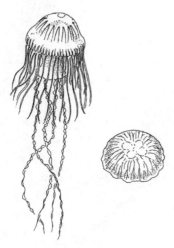

Many jellyfish are washed ashore during the summer. The compass jellyfish (left) looks impressive when floating in the water, its stinging tentacles hanging down several feet. However the common aurelia (right) is more frequently found.

(2) The beach is over 1ml/1.6km long, and is washed by mighty Atlantic rollers that pour in across the shallow bay. These are wondrous in stormy weather – originating far out at sea they roll inland, mounting higher and higher as they reach the coast. Gigantic waves crash upon the shore in thunderous roars, splashing white carpets of foam across the beach and showering the dunes in salty spray. Even though the beach environment is barren in outward appearance, it does support a complex community of plants and animals that have learned to hide from its extreme and at times violent nature. Just below low-tide level mighty forests of *kelp* stretch out

beneath the shallow water. Many of these are washed ashore in wintry gales, their long whip-like stems, some 2m long, littering the upper shoreline. However it is in winter that the real extent of the shoreline's wealth can be fully appreciated. This is when the many foreign waders make their appearance felt. Flocks of migrant *turnstones*, *plovers*, *dunlins* and *sandpipers* will be sighted as they probe the sands for food, extracting the burrowing animals with their pointed beaks. The coiled casts of some of these burrowing creatures can be seen at low tide by the water's edge. They include species such as the *lugworm* and *razor shells*. In summer the occasional *jellyfish* is found stranded by the ebbing tide. The south-west has the greater frequency of Ireland's jellyfish and you may even encounter the renowned *Portuguese man-of-war* – but be careful, as its stinging tentacles can cause major discomfort.

(3) Having walked about halfway down the beach, it is worth changing your perspective on the sea by climbing up onto the dunes and walking along the path encountered on the top of the first ridge. This runs the full length of and parallel to the beach. Dunes are quite rare as a habitat,

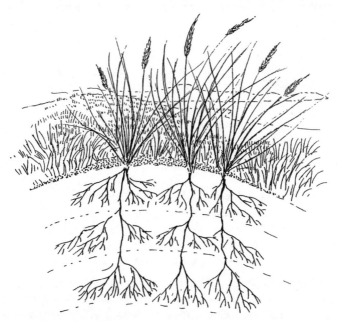

Marram grass is one of the principal plants that assists in the formation of dunes. Well suited to exposure, its leaves curl inwards to prevent excess water loss.

being confined to very specific areas of the coastline where the opportunities arise for waves to deposit the fine-grained sand and shell fragments. The many plants that have colonised these areas all have their own unique modifications that help them to survive the harsh conditions. *Marram grass* is usually the dominant grass of the dunes and it is also responsible for their development. If this plant becomes buried by further layers of sand it just grows up through it, sprouts a whole new system of roots and abandons the older ones lower down. Thus with time the extensive buried roots tie the sand together and allows it to grow up into massive mounds. Also the marram grass leaves can curl in on themselves to avoid excess water loss during dry weather.

The yellow petals of the sea-pansy make it instantly recognisable. It thrives in the salty dry sands of the dunes.

(4) If you decide to walk through the dunes you will encounter many of the characteristic coastal flora. The *sea-holly*, with its protective spiked leaves, throws up purple flowers during the months of July and August. Carpets of yellow *sea-pansy* can occur between May and September, while the yellow tufts of the *kidney vetch* may be spotted earlier in May and June. Butterflies and moths are also frequent visitors to the sheltered valleys, or dune slacks, between the dunes and you should be able to discern the striking black and red-spotted *burnet* during fine summer weather. This *six-spotted burnet* makes silky cocoons on the stems of the *marram grass* in which the larva undergoes metamorphosis into the brightly coloured adult. The scarlet red colour acts as a warning to birds, indicating a distasteful nature. Other unique inhabitants of the dunes are the *orchids*, some of which can take up to ten years before they eventually flower and seed, so please do not be tempted to pick these fragile and delicate plants.

(5) On arriving at the end of the dunes the 'long strand river' is met. Do not cross but swing LEFT back into the dunes walking towards the road. Exit out onto the road where easiest and walk carefully up to the next RIGHT turn which has a picturesque stone cottage at its entrance.

(6) On arriving at the stone cottage take the adjacent laneway that goes up on the RIGHT. NOTE: A considerable portion of the laneway floods during high spring tides in March and September. Then one must detour and take the tarred road to point (10). See map.

(7) The laneway winds its way up between the woods on the left and the reed fringed Kilkeran Lake on the right. The lane can be very muddy after rain and one gate with a stile will be met. The wide expanse of water is home to many *waterhens* that use the reeds as nesting sites. There may also be a few occasional *swans*, but other than that little bird life is seen on the open water.

The red-spotted burnet is strikingly coloured, with its red spots adorning the black fore-wings. Very different from the ugly black larva that pupates in the cocoon.

(8) Further up, the woods end and the laneway changes into a grass-covered track. This is bordered by an old stone wall on the left, the first visible signs of the Castle Freke demesne. On the right the lake disappears as it becomes choked by the enormous thickets of *reed*. These begin to send up new shoots at the end of the summer and reach a height of 2m by August, when they start to produce seed heads. They provide nesting sites for the little *sedge warbler*, whose melodious song is not quickly forgotten.

(9) The old laneway eventually becomes enclosed by hedgerows of *hawthorn* and *elm* that in early spring are alive with common songbirds such as the *blackbird*, *robin* and *thrush*. When the coniferous woods reappear on the left, the reed beds begin to thin out and are replaced by the large tufts of *tussock grass* that grow beneath the *alder trees* on the right. On the branches of these water-loving trees are great clumps of *polypody fern*, many of which grow exceedingly large because of the moist and sheltered conditions. The shady conditions also allow large numbers of ferns to grow along the track, such as *hart's tongue*, *hard fern*, *polypody* and *buckler fern*. Some wildflowers will also be encountered, with the white *wood anemone* appearing as early as March, while the *red campion* may still be flowering as late as

September. NOTE: Recent clear-felling has made the remainder of the path extremely muddy, thus wellingtons are necessary, especially after rain.

(10) The laneway finally passes a bungalow on the left and then emerges onto a tarred road through a timber gate with a stile. CROSS the road to the delightful lodge entrance opposite which is the former entrance to the Castle Freke estate. The lodge is now a private residence and the avenue has become a main road, following the abandonment of the estate earlier this century. Enter through the limestone pillars and follow the old avenue (road) up through the coniferous trees.

(11) About 200m beyond the lodge on the first bend take the rough and muddy track that leaves the road on the RIGHT. This area has been clear-felled as of 2004, thus it is in a mess and very muddy after rain. One needs to watch one's footing here but keep going STRAIGHT towards the green fields visible through the distant trees.

(12) The track becomes very indistinct but make for the green fields visible ahead. On coming near the boundary fence turn to the RIGHT and walk towards the large pine tree, a *Monterey cypress*. The area has been clear-felled and is therefore covered in a mass of invading briars, however with care one should reach the tree. The area was the former demesne shrubbery, therefore there are several large specimen trees visible amidst the remaining choked woodland.

(13) At the large pine tree go up to your LEFT through the trees, swinging RIGHT a little further up. This brings you onto another abandoned avenue of the old estate, noticeable by the thick stone walls.

(14) When you are on this overgrown avenue, go LEFT. Stay near to the left-hand side. After a thicket of *laurels* and *briars*, which you climb through, the path opens out again, passing alongside an old orchard wall. At the base of this wall, the winter-flowering *heliotrope* grows in dense tufts, its pale lilac flower-heads appearing in January and February.

(15) The old avenue connects up to another forest track. Go RIGHT, passing around the metal barrier pole and follow the track that passes up through the recently clear-felled forest. The trees shortly merge into a young *beech wood* that is very colourful when visited in autumn.

(16) At the top of the wood the road swings sharply around to the left, with another track branching off to the right. Go LEFT and continue on

Castle Freke stands imposingly amongst the trees and must have been a splendid mansion in its day.

through the plantation until a clearing is met.

(17) On reaching the clearing, follow the track down to the carpark. Here many of the trees have been cut, and good views open up across the valley and down towards the coast. Galley Head is visible to the left with its lighthouse, while to the right can be seen the spires of the ruined Rathbarry Church. A little bit to the right of the church are the remains of Rathbarry Castle, partly hidden by the trees. Recent replanting of the felled forest may block this view.

(18) On reaching the carpark, turn to the LEFT and follow the exit track down to a T-junction. As you enter the carpark the entrance to the eighteenth-century mansion of the Evans-Freke family is straight in front of you. However, this is private property and one needs permission to enter. Castle Freke was built by the prosperous Sir John Evans-Freke in 1790 and continued as the family seat up until the First World War. These powerful landlords first lived in the older Rathbarry Castle before building their splendid castellated mansion. Here they lived a life of opulence and grandeur until the arrival of the last in the line, the tenth Lord Carbery, who was by all accounts an eccentric. He abandoned the title and the house after the war, emigrating to Kenya.

Before he left, he stood at the bottom of the stairs and shot out the eyes of the portrait of the first Lord Carbery, which hung at the top of the staircase. He then walked out the door, turned the key and never returned. The house and some of the estate was eventually bought locally and the house allowed to fall rapidly into a ruin. Much of the remainder of the estate was bought by the government, its beautiful woods being cut down and replanted with conifers. The area around the mansion gives fine views over Rosscarbery Bay.

(19) At the junction go to the RIGHT along the main road for several metres, until you reach a small bridge with a metal barrier pole on your LEFT. Pass through the stile on the left-hand side of the pole and follow the track up through the newly planted conifer wood for about 500 metres until a grassy T-junction is met.

(20) On reaching the junction in the track take the LEFT path as it rises up to the ruined Rathbarry Church. Take note of the right path here, which you must return to after visiting the church ruins.

(21) Near the top you will have to swing RIGHT into some remaining trees and go through a stone stile to get into the well-kept churchyard. Having visited the church, return to the junction at point 20.This church was a fine stone-cut structure, built in 1825 to replace an older one that can be traced back to the thirteenth century. The church was abandoned in 1927 when the last baron left. Around the church are some tombs of the former gentry, who are probably responsible for the mosaic inscription on the back inside wall of the church, which reads 'until he comes'. From the front of the church can be seen the ruins of Rathbarry Castle.

(20) Having returned to the original T-junction keep going STRAIGHT and follow the muddy path through the thickets of bamboo until the tarred road is reached again. Over to the left and hidden in the trees is the recently restored Rathbarry Castle. This is private property, and not accessible to the public. It was here the Frekes originally lived, having bought the castle from the then Lord Barrymore in 1641. The castle was built by Randal Oge Barrymore in the fifteenth century, on the site of a former earthen fort. It was besieged and burned many times during the confederate wars of the seventeenth century. The second baron found the place so dilapidated in the 1780s that he abandoned it and built the new Castle Freke.

(22) On reaching the tarred road a stream must be crossed at the exit.

Once on the road follow it down to the LEFT and take the second forest track on the left.

(23) On reaching the second forest track on the LEFT, with its large wide entrance, pass around the metal barrier pole and follow the track as it climbs up the hill through the coniferous wood until a Y-junction is reached.

Excellent views of the Freke mansion will become visible behind you as you climb upwards.

(24) Further up the hill, a Y junction in the path is reached. Take the RIGHT fork and follow it upwards until a large stone cross is met at the top of the hill.

(25) On reaching the impressive cross, go STRAIGHT ahead and locate a muddy path that follows the boundary stone wall down to the LEFT.

The view from the cross is spectacular, with Galley Head and its delightful lighthouse stretching out to sea on the left. Behind are the wonderful ruins of Castlefreke. The cross itself has the most delightful carvings on its stem, with its story clearly etched into its base.

(26) Following the path by the wall, downhill, it re-enters the wood where a Y-fork is reached. Go to the RIGHT at the fork and follow the well-worn path down the muddy slope to reach the car park at the start of the walk. This path is shared with horse-riding enthusiasts, so one should watch one's footing as one descends.

# 6 – Lough Hyne

OF ALL THE REGIONS AROUND THE IRISH COASTLINE none is more dramatic than that series of peninsulas that characterise the south-west corner of the country. Not alone does the mix of mountain and sea impress itself on you, but the very nature of its formation has an equally compelling impact. Here you can read into and witness the changing face of planet earth itself, as the rise in sea levels, with the subsequent drowning of continents that has slowly but always been taking place, continues unabated. The coastal scenery near Baltimore offers an ideal opportunity to experience this strange phenomenon, which today is more commonly understood as the 'greenhouse effect'. The planet is at present in a warming-up cycle, which began about ten thousand years ago. Thus the extensive ice sheets that covered Ireland and Northern Europe melted, to result in much of our coastline being drowned in the intervening period by the resultant increase in sea levels. This cut off the land bridges which joined Ireland to Britain and mainland Europe about seven thousand years ago. Then about three thousand years later the waters reached the region around Baltimore, at the same time drowning the neighbouring glaciated valleys between the mountain chains of Shehy, Caha, the Macgillycuddy Reeks and Slieve Mish. In this way the much-loved peninsulas of Mizen, Bere, Iveragh and Dingle were formed, with their wide parallel sea inlets of Bantry, Kenmare and Dingle bays.

Today it is very easy to detect the outline of this drowned landscape as it still protrudes above the rising ocean flood. Craggy peaks of former mountain tops are reduced to sea-lashed islands now separated from the mainland, while the higher mountain chains have remained to probe finger-like, as towering peninsulas, out into the western Atlantic, their sides spliced into precipitous sea cliffs. It is amidst the turmoil of this eroded coastline that the fascinating Lough Hyne – the only inland sea lake in Europe – is found. Once a fresh-water lake, it too has succumbed to the rising sea. Thus at high tide its water surface is below sea level, causing the river to flow inland! At low tide it is above, allowing its emerging river to flow seaward in a raging, noisy torrent.

A strange twist of geography has thus shaped this great sea basin on land making it one of the true magical treasures of the south-west, and a rarity in Europe. The lough, since its submergence many years ago, has developed into an immense and unique marine aquarium that gives us a window into deep oceanic life where many rare and unusual species abound that are not really native to Ireland. Truly a rare spot that well deserved the honour of being Ireland's first marine nature reserve.

## WALK DESCRIPTION

LOCATION: Well-signposted turn-off 2.5ml/4km west of Skibbereen on the Baltimore road. A further 2.5ml/4km leads straight to Lough Hyne.

TERRAIN: Mostly a walk along quiet country by-roads that skirt Lough Hyne's wooded shoreline and upland heath, giving fine sea views.

FEATURES: Lough Hyne's shoreline, oak and beech woods, Barloge creek, heathland, ringfort, Atlantic ocean views and drowned coastline.

LENGTH: 4ml/6.5km.

TIME: 2.5 hours.

EQUIPMENT: comfortable walking shoes; binoculars would be an advantage.

## WALK OUTLINE

(1) As soon as you reach the lough you are at the very small roadside layby, beneath the beautiful wooded slopes of Knockomagh Wood. Do read the interpretative sign located here before beginning the walk as it

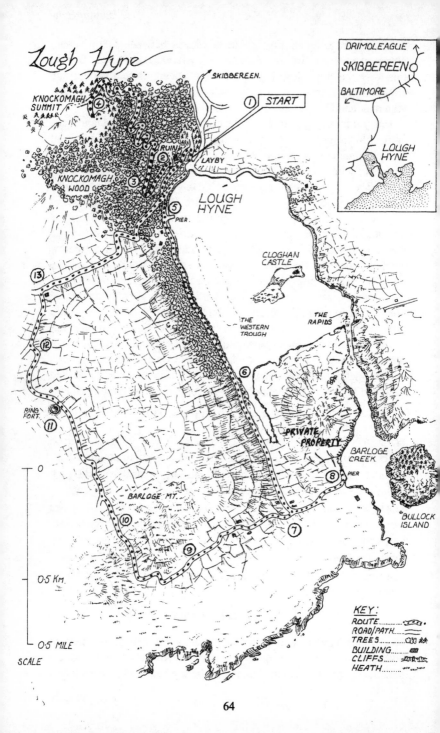

Lough Hyne

SKIBBEREEN.

KNOCKOMAGH SUMMIT ④

KNOCKOMAGH WOOD

① START

LAYBY

RUIN ②

③

⑤ PIER

LOUGH HYNE

CLOGHAN CASTLE

THE WESTERN TROUGH

THE RAPIDS

⑬

⑫

RING FORT. ⑪

⑥

PRIVATE PROPERTY

BARLOGE CREEK

PIER ⑧

BULLOCK ISLAND

0

BARLOGE MT.

⑩

⑨

⑦

0·5 Km.

0·5 MILE

SCALE

DRIMOLEAGUE ↑

SKIBBEREEN ○

BALTIMORE ←

LOUGH HYNE

KEY:
ROUTE .......
ROAD/PATH .......
TREES .......
BUILDING .......
CLIFFS .......
HEATH .......

64

gives a very good explanation of the lough's ecology. At the layby and facing the interpretative sign go to the RIGHT, the path running up beside a small stream and into the *coniferous wood*. Pass through the timber stile and very shortly take the path that branches off to the LEFT. This has a sign for the 'hill top' nailed to a tree.

(2) The path very quickly climbs steeply uphill after which a junction is met. Take the signposted path up to the RIGHT. Soon you will reach a ruined stone cottage on the right, but watch for the obscure path as it branches up to the LEFT opposite the cottage. Knockomagh Wood is a fine old *oak* and *beech wood* that has now also been protected with nature reserve status.

(3) After the cottage the path continues to rise steeply upwards by another series of steps. At the top of these steps watch for the evergreen yew trees above your head. These are remnant trees of the ancient forest that once cloaked these hills. Their presence is significant in that it indicates that Knockomagh Wood is a lot older than is generally realised, and is not a planted wood of the eighteenth century, even though some planting of *beech* did occur then. There is a possibility that this wood has been present here, uninterrupted, for several thousand years and is more correctly described as aboriginal. Good vistas of the lough open up from time to time showing its sheltered position and its proximity to the sea. Later, another path branches off to the right, but ignore it and continue on up STRAIGHT.

(4) Many more steps help the ascent, as you pass through delightful groves of *beech* and *oak*. The ground under these trees is covered in rich swards of *ivy, pennywort, wood sorrel, herb robert, fern* and *wood rush*. At times, especially in the autumn, you will surely spot the colourful orange leaves of the *spindle tree*, another rare specimen of south-west Ireland that is usually associated with ancient woodlands, such as the Gearagh near Macroom. Finally you come near the summit where the path opens out into a clearing surrounded by *furze* and *heather*. Here it divides as a Y-fork; go to the LEFT. Follow the path out to the rocky ridge where you will have a fine view out over the entire lough and the surrounding coastline. The right fork in the path leads to the true summit of Knockomagh, but this is becoming enclosed by conifers that block out the views.

(5) Retrace your steps back down to the junction just beyond the ruined cottage at point (2). Go to the RIGHT and follow the path down onto the tarred road. Here the road forks but take the LEFT branch down through

This yew is a native of the ancient woods and the tree has a different shape to the more familiar introduced yew found in graveyards and gardens.

the wooded roadside and around the shoreline to pass the pier on your left. Soon you are on a delightful stretch of roadside, overhung with *oak* and *beech*. In spring, this woodland floor becomes covered with rich growths of *wood sorrel*, *bluebell* and *primrose*. These forest flowers have to blossom before the leaves appear on the upper canopy and block out all available light to the ground, and they have thus evolved a life cycle that allows them to co-exist with other species rather than having to compete with them. Notice how the roadside drops steeply into the water on your left. You are now passing the lough's deepest part, The Western Trough, which is over 130ft/40m deep!

Peering across the water through the trees, watch for the island towards the opposite side. The ruins of Cloghan Castle, now a pile of ivy-clad stones, form its highest point. This was an old O'Driscoll defensive tower-house that protected the entrance into the lough. It offered a safe haven for their ships, when travelling up and down the coastline in the fifteenth century – which was much safer than trekking through the densely forested interior of the country. The castle is also said to be the legendary home of King Labhra Loingseach, who, according to the legend, had the ears of an ass – a secret he guarded closely, putting to death any barber who cut his hair! One such misfortunate barber, however, had to rid himself of the bizarre secret before he died and he whispered it to a nearby tree. In time the tree was cut down and a passing bard on his way to the castle asked the tree-cutter for a piece to make a harp. The harp was made and the bard eventually arrived at the castle. But when he began to play, the only tune it would play was: *'Tá dhá cluais asail ar an Rí Labhra Loingseach'* (King Labhra Loingseach has the ears of an ass). All the trees of the surrounding woods joined in and, overwhelmed with shame, the king fled never to be seen again!

(6) On emerging from the trees you will pass a sign on your left for the Lough Hyne Reserve's Marine Research Station. It is from here that the numerous Irish and foreign marine biologists embark to carry out their research around the lough. Using diving gear, which now requires a permit from the government, the incredible wealth beneath the waters can be observed. Exotic and weird *red-mouthed goby fish, trigger fish, tompot blemy fish, pipefish, sponges, sea squirts, coral, fan worms, luminous jellyfish* and strange spider-like *crabs* – all traverse the deep waters to astound and delight the

Seaweeds vary enormously in appearance, but all have a characteristic holdfast that anchors them to immobile rocks, allowing their fronds to float free. Left to right: kelp, bladder wrack, thong weed.

scientists. Several thousand species occur, some coming from as far away as Portugal and the Mediterranean. The richness of this lake is unrivalled anywhere else in Ireland or Britain.

(7) Leaving the waters of the reserve behind, follow the fuchsia-clad hedgerows until you come to the next junction. Go LEFT, around and behind the buildings, to follow the road down to Barloge Pier. *Fuchsia* is not an original native plant, having been imported from south America in times past, thus it supports very little wildlife compared to our native hedgerow *hawthorn* bush.

(8) On arriving at the pier you will be looking out onto Barloge Creek. This is usually full of the black,

Many of the shelled animals remain dormant and immobile until the tide turns: (a) limpet (b) acorn barnacles (c) saddle oyster.

The bright, multicoloured – red, black, blue, yellow – wings of the native
peacock butterfly make it easy to spot.

diving *shags*, with only their scrawny necks poking out of the water.
Around the shoreline rocks stand grey-white *herons*, poking for crab
and fish that become stranded by the falling tide. To your right is the exit
to the sea, straight in front is the cave-riddled Bullock Island, while to
your left is the entrance to the lough. The creek is shallow and well
sheltered from the ocean, thus it supports extensive mats of rarer *sea
grass* rather than the more usual seaweeds. The route must now retrace
its steps back up to the last junction at point (7).

(7) Arriving back at this junction, go to the LEFT, rising up the steep hill
and past a number of farm houses. Their surrounding small meadows
are delightful in summer when the hay grows. Many of the
characteristic wildflowers will be spotted amongst the high grass,
painting a colourful canvas of reds, yellows and whites. Look for
*ox-eye daisies*, *clovers* and *buttercups*.

(9) This route takes you up and over Barloge Mountain, full of the
*dwarf autumn gorse* and common *heather*, a blaze of yellow and purple
in late summer and autumn. Watch for *stonechats* and *wheatears* in the
bracken – these are small birds that are more common around our
western coast and not usually seen inland. *Tortoise-shell*, *red admiral*
and *peacock butterflies* abound among the heathland flowers, the rough
moorland having escaped the scourge of pesticides from intensive
farming.

Looking out to sea excellent views of the Atlantic ocean stretch away
south towards the coast of Spain. On your left you should be able to see

the Stag's Rock, a wave-lashed pinnacle, and all that remains of this former mountaintop which was originally part of the mainland several thousand years ago.

(10) Follow the road UP over the summit of the mountain until the wide expanse of Roaring Water Bay, with its many islands, comes into view. This archipelago was once a cluster of hills, deposited by glaciers on an ancient and extensive grassy tundra. The valley sides of this drowned plain are now represented by the Mizen Peninsula away to the right and the islands of Cape Clear and Sherkin, hidden behind Baltimore, to your left. Cape Clear and Sherkin are in fact the unsubmerged peaks of the former mountain chain that now runs out under the sea.

(11) Continue on DOWNHILL, ignoring any turn-offs and after 1km. watch for a fine earthen ring-fort, on the brow of a hill and against the left wall (just before the bungalows). This is the remains of an ancient dwelling, common in neolithic times. Around it runs an excellent example of the deep trench or fosse, that was usually filled with water and served for defence purposes, protecting inhabitants from wolves during the early Bronze Age. Inside the earthen wall was a simple wattle and clay house that had a thatched roof. Better views of Sherkin and Cape Clear islands can also be seen from here, with Clear's two hydroelectric windmills visible on a clear day. The windmills are part of a modern energy experiment that was carried out to investigate the feasibility of tapping wind power as a source of electricity. Ireland's western coastline is constantly hit by blustery south-westerly winds and it should therefore have marvellous potential for exploiting this clean and renewable energy source. Highly successful on a small scale, further research for large-scale

In early summer you may spot the first arrival of the red admiral which will have flown all the way from the Continent. It rests on sunny rocks about the upland heath.

69

application was hampered by lack of funding. Away to the right you should be able to see the two multifaceted white domes of the air-tracking station, monitoring all overhead flights, on Mizen's highest peak, Mount Gabriel.

(12) Follow the road to the next T-junction and go RIGHT. From here on be prepared to meet the occasional few cars, especially during the summer tourist season.

(13) Pass the farm entrance on your right and go on to the next T-junction, where you turn RIGHT by the cottage to arrive back at Lough Hyne and the carpark (5) and (1).

# 7 – Sheep's Head

STANDING ON THE TIP OF THE 'SHEEP'S HEAD', the collision of land and sea is experienced in all its abandoned extremity. One of the south-west's characteristic peninsulas, it juts far out into the Atlantic and has all the attributes of an offshore island. Although this exposes it to the full onslaught of ocean gales that can give it a bleak and barren appearance during wet and windy weather, it is an area that is quite unique in several respects. It may not have the high peaks and corried valleys of the other peninsulas, but the Sheep's Head, being West Cork's most isolated peninsula, can boast the purest and wildest coastal scenery in all of the south-west. No roads traverse its wilderness, no gaudy consumerism mars its purity, and no barbed-wire fences block the walker's way. The winds, scented of yellow gorse and purple heath, buffet about its creviced glens and rocky outcrops.

Around the coast, many thousands of birds return from months at sea each spring to nest and feed their young. Here they breed in great colonies on the many neighbouring cliffs that shield the mainland and offshore islands. Come the autumn, many passing migrant birds graze the coastline as they return from northern Europe to the African continent, taking one last breath on Irish soil before heading down across the Atlantic.

Surrounded by uninterrupted views of the mighty ocean, the Sheep's Head commands excellent vistas across one of the best places in Europe to spot cetaceans, those wonderful creatures of the sea that are now facing the final onslaught of extinction. These are the *whales, porpoises* and *dolphins* that annually pass up and down the Irish coastline as they migrate between the northern Atlantic and the equatorial regions of southern latitudes, moving up in the spring and down in the autumn. They are regularly sighted every year, with many unfortunately becoming beached around the coast, dying a horrible death as they become fouled in discarded fishing nets or injured by passing boats.

In summer, cool fresh breezes brush the heathery hills as rolling blue skies drift across the empty wilderness; *skylarks* sing hanging in the air while *gannets* in their hundreds plummet arrow-like into the sea. Images that remain with you long after walking along the elevated coastline of the Sheep's Head and that will call you to return again and again to the many unadulterated wilderness areas of West Cork.

Welcome to one of my, and West Cork's, best-kept walking secrets.

## WALK DESCRIPTION

LOCATION: Travel 2mls/3.2km on the N71 from Bantry to Ballydehob and take the R591 regional road for Durrus on your RIGHT. Having travelled 4mls/6.5km to the village of Durrus, go to the RIGHT at the sign-posted Y-junction in the village and follow the coastal road for 9.5mls/15km, to the cosy hamlet of Kilcrohane. Passing through Kilcrohane, follow the road for another 2.8mls/4.5km until a distinct Y-junction is reached in the townland of Caher. At the junction there is a stone house on the left and another large house up on your right. Just beyond the junction there is a small lay-by on the LEFT where you can park safely.

TERRAIN: A spectacular, long but very tough walk that crosses over wild heaths, passes through empty glens and along some SERIOUSLY HIGH CLIFFS within the more remote parts of the peninsula. It is DEFINITELY NOT FOR THE INEXPERIENCED, as one passes through much uninhabited terrain. Therefore if weather conditions deteriorate or you sustain an injury you will not be able to call for help.

WARNING: Never travel it alone and only with those who know how to deal with unexpected conditions and can administer first aid. Also, in

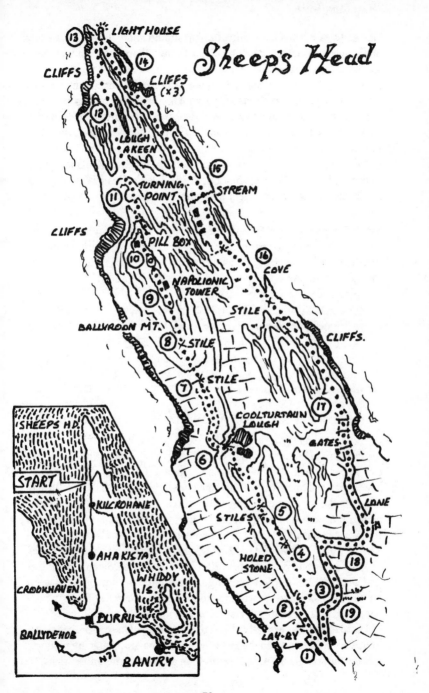

Sheep's Head

LIGHTHOUSE
CLIFFS
CLIFFS (x3)
LOUGH AKEEN
TURNING POINT
STREAM
CLIFFS
PILL BOX
COVE
NAPOLIONIC TOWER
STILE
BALLYROON MT.
CLIFFS.
STILE
STILE
COOLTURTAUN LOUGH
GATES
STILES
LONE
HOLED STONE

SHEEPS HD
START
KILCROHANE
AHAKISTA
WHIDDY IS.
CROOKHAVEN
DURRUS
BALLYDEHOB
N71
BANTRY

LAY-BY

73

case of thick coastal fog rolling in, you should know how to read maps and compasses and be EXPERIENCED enough to find your way back safely. Over-enthusiastic beginners have ignored such warnings in the past and regretted it dearly. This has resulted in some of the walks featured in previous editions of this book being closed off by distressed land-owners. In the long term, carelessness by a minority of naive, inexperienced walkers erodes all walkers' access to the outdoors. Please be sensible.

FEATURES: Wonderful cliff scenery, rocky heath and blanket bog; Sheep's Head lighthouse; the delightful Sheep's Head Way; old bog roads and laneways; excellent panoramas of the surrounding coast.

DISTANCE: 10mls/16km.

TIME: 7 hours or more. Because of the length and the tough terrain, one needs to have time to spare and be able to afford lots of rests. It is also nice to have the time to appreciate the exquisite wild flora and to absorb the many commanding views of West Cork's incredible mountainous and peninsular topography.

EQUIPMENT: Strong, waterproof hiking boots with a good grip and ankle support; knapsack to carry food, liquid and extra clothing, including rain wear. Compass and maps, including both the OS Discovery series no. 88 and the Sheep's Head Way map and guide book. Additional information can be obtained from the Sheep's Head Way committee, Kealties, Durrus.

## WALK OUTLINE

(1) From the lay-by follow the road west by going to the LEFT. Ignore the tarred road branching off to the left further up and continue to follow the 'Sheep's Head Way' walking signs for another few hundred metres, keeping an eye open for two adjacent lanes branching off to your RIGHT.

Along the way there are fine views across the bay to the Mizen Head peninsula, with its similar topography of a long spine of mountains running far out to sea. The five peninsulas of Ireland's south-west – Mizen, Sheep's Head, Beara, Iveragh and Dingle – are a parallel series of mountains and intervening valleys created by a volcanic upheaval that occured 250 million years ago. They have become greatly worn down since then and the valleys flooded by a rise in sea levels which happened at the end of the last ice age, about 6000 BC.

These factors have greatly affected the ecology of the region, causing it to be very different from the rest of Ireland. One group that are predominant in the area are the unique *Lusitanian* group of plants and animals.

(2) On reaching the two adjacent lanes, take the first one by using the stile next to the iron gate and follow the lane up to another stile. Cross over the second, sign-posted stile into a field (very muddy after rain) and follow the fence up to another stile and gate near a stone building.

(3) Cross over this third stile and follow the adjacent laneway (up to your right) as it heads LEFT and west into the rocky heath. A blaze of purple if seen in August, this is an old military road that travelled out to the napoleonic signal tower near the end of the peninsula. All about, the native *gorse* blooms yellow in autumn, as does the purple *heather.* Looking rather impoverished, it actually supports a great number of insects, which in turn support heathland birds like *skylarks* and *pipits.* These then become prey to native predatory birds like the *kestrel* and *merlin.*

(4) The lane eventually passes beside a two-storey house on the left and leads out to a wet, marshy area full of *rush,* with an adjacent 'Way marker'. Here the less distinct laneway leads up to a more defined path that passes up between two stone walls, at the end of which is a stepped timber stile. Crossing the stile, the 'Way' now becomes a footpath that wanders out onto some delightful wild heathland.

If very wet it helps to stay up high on the rocky heath, but you need to keep an eye on where you are going and watch for the 'Way marked' poles. Staying with these will lead you safely across the rock-splattered, boggy heath.

Before pushing on from the two-storey house you can see the locally-known 'Holed Stone'. Just beyond the house and down to the left you should be able to work your way up through some wet terrain and briars where, on the other side of a stone wall, it lies prostrate on the ground. Originally a 'standing stone', possibly of Celtic archaeological origin, its primary significance has long since disappeared. In more recent, post-Celtic times, Catholic traditions have claimed it for their own use, calling it the 'marriage stone'. The male puts his larger hand in the wider

The yellow flowers of the kidney vetch are surrounded by white hairs which attract nectar-seeking insects from June to August.

side, the female her smaller hand in the narrower. While holding hands they then make their marraige vows.

(5) When you encounter and pass the outline of a low stone wall on your LEFT, you presently arrive at another stepped foot stile and, shortly beyond it, a foot stile over a barbed-wire fence. Having crossed both stiles, follow the 'Way poles' west, keeping the wire fence on your right.

As you traverse the grassy heath, *stonechats* and *wheatears* will be seen moving around the rocky tussocks. The *wheatears'* numbers increase during the autumn and spring migrations.

(6) Eventually the wild heath comes to an end and the path descends down to another stepped, timber stile that leads out onto a tarred road. Follow the road to the LEFT for a few metres and take the next RIGHT turn-off, following the road up between some houses and eventually back onto another wonderful stretch of the original military road.

Just to the right of the stepped stile there are some beautiful fresh-water lakes awash with wild nature. Their edges are crowded with expansive sheets of water-loving flora, while their surfaces are blanketed in *water lilies*. About the vegetation, large *Aeshnea* and *Four-spotted Libula* dragonflies scout the air for other insect prey, such as *damselflies*. The presence of both these insect varieties indicates the purity of these waters, as their aquatic larval stages are very intolerant of pollution.

(7) Following the old military road west, another fence with a stile crosses the track, after which the 'Way' leads out onto some incredible wild heath, towering above the crashing waves far below. Eventually the track peters out and reverts to a path as you begin the ascent of Ballyroon mountain. Here a foot stile leads you over a barbed-wire fence. Continue to follow the 'Way marked' poles up and out along the creviced peak of Ballyroon mountain, until you eventually encounter the shattered remains of the old napoleonic signal-tower.

If you stray from the main route it is very easy to get lost out here, so be careful. There are a number of abandoned dwellings and tiny meadows, that appear to be of a pre-Famine origin, scattered among the south-facing rocky glens. On a sunny day it seems a most romantic place to live, but during the long, dark winters reality paints a different picture. Famine and deprivation would have driven most of the inhabitants to the new world.

As you follow the path you will surely be struck by the great show of summer flowers, whether they be the purple *heathers*, the yellow *bog asphodels* or the white tufts of *bog cotton*. Relatively undisturbed, the area also supports numerous butterflies, regularly encountered in the sunnier and more sheltered spots throughout the summer. In late autumn and winter the dried, spiked tufts of tall *moor grass* march across the sleepy moors, turning them a russet golden-brown – a landscape that has not yet found its painter!

(8) As you climb the rocky ridge, excellent views of the surrounding terrain open up. On your left is Dunmanus Bay, with the most southerly peninsula of Mizen Head running out to Ireland's Land's End. To the right is Bantry Bay, with the mountainous backdrop of the Beara peninsula and its wonderful Caha mountains. Hungry Hill towers above the nearby Bere Island, which can be distinguished by the white beacon at its cliffed western end.

Bantry Bay is very deep and was chosen by the British to harbour its fleet from the prying eyes of the Germans during the Second World War. They hid their ships behind Bere Island. In more recent times the bay has been chosen as the country's main oil storage depot, since the huge tankers can come right up to Whiddy Island, just offshore from Bantry town. Sadly, the tragedy of the *Betelgeuse* explosion of 1979 has left a deep scar in the minds of the local people. The oil tanker caught fire while offloading, killing several people and causing much pollution in the bay.

(9) Having reached the ruins of the old napoleonic tower, the path continues to follow the ridge UP and westwards to the OS concrete pillar. The tower stood until 1990, when a strong gale levelled it right down to its very base. It is one of several towers scattered along the coastline, and they communicated with each other by means of fires lit on top. If one spotted an enemy ship approaching, it could relay the message of danger rapidly to the other towers all along the coast, and so to military barracks in large centres like Bantry and ultimately Cork.

(10) From the OS pillar, follow the path DOWN, past the Second World War pill box and ultimately down to a carpark. There are some dangerous

The long-abandoned signal tower is one of many scattered along the headlands of the west.

cliffs ahead, so stay alert and heed the warning signs. A number of foot stiles will lead you over the fences as you proceed.

Looking back over the peninsula, the unique structure of the south-west's topography is well illuminated. From here one can see the nature of the drowned valleys and the parallel ridges, which were created like a buckled sheet of galvanised iron by the earth upheaval, or 'Armorican folding', that occured approximately 250 million years ago.

(11) On arriving down onto the carpark or 'turning point', cross it to the LEFT and follow the road down to the first bend. There you leave the road again and cross back into the heath on your RIGHT, following the outline of a footpath.

This takes you out to the tip of the Sheep's Head. This area is becoming more popular with the car-based tourist, so you will encounter several people around this spot during the summer months. Again, the cliffs surround you on all sides, so you need to exercise caution and be aware of their constant erosion in such an exposed environment. Every winter huge sections of the peninsula's end crash into the sea. BE SENSIBLE.

## OPTION

Before proceeding from the 'turning point', it is advisable to make an assessment of your progress. You have not yet reached the halfway point of the walk and there is still another good 6mls/10km to be covered, which crosses rather difficult terrain. It will take you at least another 3-4 hours to finish the walk. If you have had enough, or realise that you are running out of time, now is the time to turn back by going to the RIGHT and following the narrow roadway back to the walk's start.

(12) As you follow the path outwards, try to take a middle course, keeping well back from the cliffed left-hand side. It is constantly being eroded by the sea and the heath underfoot is unstable. It may be a fine day when you visit, but it is possible that a gale a few days previously has left the cliff-line weak. Remember that you are on the edge of the Atlantic, and waves pound this coastline each winter with a force of 20 tons per square metre.

There are some splendid views of the old red sandstone cliffs that run along the length of the headland. Splintered and torn by the pounding sea, they drop down several hundred feet to crumbled, rocky outcrops that stretch up the length of the coastline. In summer these rocks will be

From left to right: guillemot with egg; razorbill; puffin, who, like many sea-birds spend most of their lives on the sea, returning to land only to breed.

crowded with large flocks of *auk, guillemot, razorbill* and the occasional *puffin*. These are true marine birds that spend most of their life on the water, far out at sea.

As you approach the peninsula tip, you first pass another fresh water lake, Lough Akeen, on your right. Beyond this the path wanders about the rocks and leads ultimately out to the picturesque lighthouse that hangs precariously above the cliffs on the right.

(13) On reaching the peninsula's end, steps and railings lead down to the lighthouse. The lighthouse was erected in the 1960s by the oil companies in order to facilitate easy movement of the large tankers in and out of the bay. Nearby, you should also encounter a circle of white-painted stones. Can you guess what it is for?

Keep an eye out for sea birds if here in summer. In the spring and autumn you may be lucky enough to spot cetaceans, as the west coast of Ireland is on the edge of a major migratory route. Shoals of *dolphin* and *porpoise*, as well as *fin, minke, sperm, pilot, humpback* and *killer whales* are all regularly sighted. Unfortunately, with the advent of plastic, these beautiful creatures have being dying horrible deaths. Ultimately washed into the sea, bags, condoms, discarded fishing gear and many other variations of plastic are being mistaken by these large animals as squid and jellyfish and thus swallowed. These objects are indigestible and clog up the whales' digestive systems, causing them eventually to starve to death. The fact that this plastic will remain in the sea environment for at least 500 years before it breaks down makes the whole scenario even more disheartening. Of all the common products produced by modern society, plastic is the most repulsive and should be boycotted by everyone. If you find one of these misfortunate cetaceans anywhere along the coastline, report it to the nearest university.

(14) Having located and viewed the lighthouse, the path turns to the

Sea-thrift grows in tufted domes of pink flowers that withstand harsh winds and exposure to salt-laden air.

RIGHT and follows the outline of the peninsula back along its northern flank. Ahead lies the most spectacular section of the walk. It begins by passing through a rocky gorge and leads back towards the mainland through completely uninhabited country. BE WARNED OF THE ADJACENT HIGH CLIFFS THAT WILL ACCOMPANY YOU FOR THE NEXT FEW KILOMETERS. There is no short cut ahead, so make sure that you are capable of completing the journey to arrive safely at point (17). But first, read and take note of the following, then put the book in your pocket and stay alert.

'The path comes precariously close to three cliffed precipices, the first having a short length of protective railing. Stay well up amongst the more rocky terrain to the RIGHT, avoiding the more treacherous cliff line. Also watch your footing as there are numerous boulders hidden beneath the heath.'

In summer the heath is covered with a marvellous display of southern coastal plants that give the clifftops a rock-garden quality. Even though the number of plants on the west coast is poor compared to the east, those that do grow here do so in wild luxuriance. The pink *sea-thrift,*

Dolphins (top) are readily distinguishable from porpoises (bottom) by their ability to jump out of the water.

white *sea-campion* and yellow *kidney vetch* clutter the ground in large, cushion-like tufts. Look through the heather for the *wild thyme* that grows in low clusters of purple flowers about the rocks. It has a mild thyme-like scent when crushed. Higher up, purple *heathers* and the dwarf *autumn gorse* make their appearance as the true heath begins.

80

(15) When well past the more exposed cliffs, a stream crosses the path. Hereabouts, and up to your right, an abandoned settlement of stone houses will be spotted, nestled against the rocky hill. Dating from pre-Famine times, when the rural population was quite large, people were forced to eke out an existence even in the most isolated of locations.

(16) Later, as the higher cliffs are left behind, a foot stile leads over a fence and the path wanders down to a small cove of splintered rock and crashing waves. Here a waterfall spills over the low cliff and shortly beyond it a stepped stile crosses over the stream.

(17) The 'Way' now gradually rises up again, over the next heather-clad hill and back to more cultivated terrain. As you near the farmland a track is encountered. Follow this downward, passing through three gates with stiles until, just beyond a house on the right, you arrive at a T-junction. Here you go to the LEFT.

(18) Having passed a lane coming in from the left, the road arrives at another T-junction, where you go to the RIGHT. Further up the hill, the

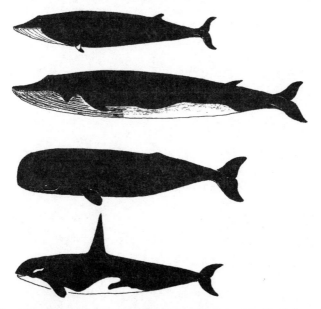

The air-breathing whales travel in shoals and can be distinguished by their spout when surfacing for air. Additionally the dorsal fin aids identification.
Top to bottom: minke, fin, sperm, killer.

Common seals (top) are distinguished from the grey by their head outline, with the grey seal having a characteristic Roman nose.

road swings LEFT around a sharp bend. At this point another road comes in on the right, but ignore it.

(19) Continue to follow the road over the hill and back to the southern side of the peninsula again. After a mile or so you arrive at the initial Y-junction of the walk's start. Once there, swing to the RIGHT to arrive at the lay-by and the parked car.

# 8 – Priest's Leap

THE HIGH MOUNTAINS THAT CHARACTERISE Ireland's south-west are so extensive in their mass that, at times, it is hard to comprehend their impact on the region. It is very much a case of not being able to see the woods for the trees. Thus without having to be an experienced mountain climber it is enjoyable to be able to climb to the top of a well-positioned peak and absorb the vista of the entire landscape as it unfolds beneath you. Such an opportunity presents itself on the western border of Cork, above the shores of Bantry Bay. Located within the Shehy Mountains is West Cork's highest peak, Knockboy, towering up over the region at 2321ft/700m. Below, a three-dimensional 'map' of the mountainous and peninsular south-west stretches around the full 360 degrees, and here you get a total view of the entire West Cork landscape as well as views into Kerry. Constantly switching colour with the seasons, the wild uplands present themselves in an ever-changing kaleidoscope of colour that is never the same on any two visits. In summer, purples and greens blanket the hills, while in autumn the silver-grey, lichened rocks merge with the sweeping drifts of russet-brown bracken, both sliding down the lower slopes to meet the faded, yellow-green fields. Abandoned stone walls and cabins of pre-famine farms abound and all about the stony silence is muted by the sound of a perpetual murmur that echoes up from the many streams cascading across the valley floor. Such wild, abandoned silence offers the utmost in peace and tranquillity.

## WALK DESCRIPTION

LOCATION: 7ml/11km from Bantry. Travelling on the main road from Bantry to Glengarriff, pass through Ballylickey and take the first RIGHT turn 1.5ml/2km after the Ovane Falls Inn. Keep a careful eye out for this small road which has a signpost for Kilgarvan. Travel for 1ml/1.6km to the Coomhola bridge where there is a shop- cum-postoffice. Do not cross the bridge, but go LEFT and then RIGHT. Travel STRAIGHT for another 1ml/1.6km, parking your car when you come to the last electricity pole, just beyond the last house.

TERRAIN: The greater part of the walk is easy, following a good mountain track that climbs up to the Priest's Leap. From here, there is an OPTION available that climbs to the top of Knockboy. This crosses the uplands which are wet, rocky and moderately strenuous. Thus it should be attempted in clear, fine weather only. NOTE: Several sheep wire fences will have to be crossed in order to arrive at the summit of Knockboy. Cross these with care and consideration.

FEATURES: Glaciated valley, pre-famine farm holdings, mountainous uplands and its associated wildlife, Priest's Leap, West Cork's highest peak (Knockboy), panoramic views of West Cork.

LENGTH: 5.5ml/8.8km. The OPTION is 2.5ml/4km extra.

TIME: 3 hours. The OPTION takes 1 hour extra.

EQUIPMENT: Strong walking boots, with waterproof boots or wellingtons being desirable for the OPTION. No dogs please.

## WALK DESCRIPTION

(1) Arriving at the last of the houses and electricity poles, in the townland of Carran, park the car sensibly and walk STRAIGHT uphill along the tarred road. This is part of an old road that goes right over the mountaintop into Kerry, a short cut that connected Bantry to Kenmare. Many of these tracks that straddle the mountains were once important routes of commerce for the subsistence farmers that lived among the soil-impoverished foothills, during the eighteenth and nineteenth centuries. They would have been little more than horse tracks and footpaths, thus they were never suitable for improvement with the

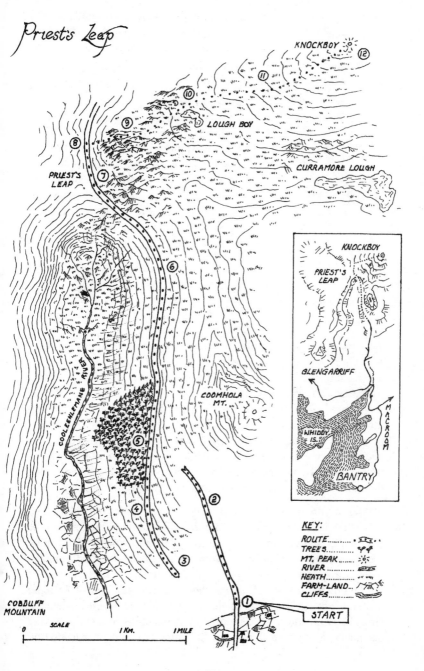

Priest's Leap

KNOCKBOY

⑫

⑪

⑩

⑨

⑰ LOUGH BOY

⑧

PRIEST'S
LEAP

⑦

CURRAMORE LOUGH

⑥

COOLEENLEMANE RIVER

COOMHOLA
MT.

⑤

④

②

③

KNOCKBOY

PRIEST'S
LEAP

GLENGARRIFF

MACROOM

WHIDDY
IS.

BANTRY

KEY:
ROUTE............ •ᴛᴛᴛ• •
TREES............ ♈♉
MT. PEAK....... ☀
RIVER ............ ⌇⌇⌇
HEATH............ ᴠⁱⁱ ᴠⁱⁱ
FARM-LAND... 🗠🗠
CLIFFS............ ⌒⌒⌒

①

START

COBDUFF
MOUNTAIN

SCALE

0            1 KM.        1 MILE

85

advent of the modern twentieth-century car, though they are still used by the surrounding sheep farmers.

(2) Further up, the tarred road becomes an earthen track, its edges bordered by boulders and sheep-wire fencing. In summer the road margins will be full of the small but curious *eyebright*, a delicate plant with tiny, tubular white flowers. The old people were well aware of the powers of this plant, using it as an eye wash for sore and itchy eyes, a problem often encountered as a result of the smoke from the turf fires within their cabins.

Eyebright, only a few inches high, will be found growing abundantly all through the summer.

(3) As you gain height above the valley, the tall, rock-streaked ridge of Curraghgarbh rises up on your left. The strips of clefted rock that protrude through the heath lie in characteristic lines, illustrating the sedimentation layers that occurred when these rocks were being formed over four hundred million years ago. This entire landscape was very different then – a billowing hot arid desert, subjected to sporadic and violent flash floods that formed temporary but expansive freshwater seas. Here the sand became sedimented and later compressed into the characteristic old red sandstone of the south-west. When the landscape folded 250 million years later, the various sedimented layers of rock were twisted into the odd shapes we can see in the mountains today. These layers were further exposed by the glacial action that occurred here up to ten thousand years ago, as it carved out this U-shaped valley.

(4) Below you the small Cooleenlemane river tumbles over blackened rocks that protrude through the thin soil of the valley floor. Along the river banks and running up the sides of the steep-sided valley can be seen a number of abandoned stone-walled fields. Nestled amongst them are a few square stone-walled enclosures, the remains of pre-famine farmsteads. Life for these people was one of extreme hardship, always bordering on the verge of starvation. Thus when the Great Famine came in 1845 these tiny but numerous communities were decimated. Many made it as far as the nearest port and managed to find

freedom in either America or Australia. So it is from areas like this that a vast number of the early Irish immigrants originated.

(5) Rising steeply upwards, the road eventually passes an evergreen wood of *Scots pine* on the left. Strangely isolated in the otherwise barren valley, these trees are part of an old reforestation programme. But they are unique in that they illustrate what the original vegetation that once grew here looked like. Prior to the seventeenth century, these valleys were full of yew, arbutus, oak and pine trees that hid the red and fallow deer. Today the sheep replace the deer, eating everything with a thoroughness that will ensure the continued sterility of the mountain vegetation as they prevent the regeneration of the trees with new seedlings. Watch for the *sparrow hawks* in the treetops. They make the most of their isolated vantage point, spying out the *meadow pipits*

Sparrow-hawks are excellent birds for chasing out and catching their prey. Once caught in the grip of their talons there is no escape.

and *skylarks* and thus keeping their numbers in check. More commonly sighted though is the croaking, grey and black *hooded crow*, which thrives on the carrion of dead sheep and other animals.

Until recently the road reverted to a delightful earthen track at this point, keeping cars at bay. However, as of 1998 the county council has repaired the remainder of the road and opened it up to traffic. Unfortunately, this will ruin its tranquillity as a walking route and destroy the very reason why people like to come up here. Hopefully it will not get totally overrun with sedentary summer tourists.

(6) As one nears the top of the mountain pass, the raucous call of the *raven* becomes more audible. These large black birds nearly always fly in pairs, as they mate for life like the swan. Beautiful birds in flight, they can be seen soaring high up above. They are early breeders, building

their nests on an inaccessible cliff ledge from February onwards. At one time these birds were kept as court pets by the old Irish chieftains. It was a raven that landed on the shoulder of the well-known Irish hero Cúchulainn, who lived in the first century BC. He was mortally wounded in a battle, the famous Táin Bó Cuailgne, against Maeve, Queen of Connacht, over a champion bull. His opponents realised he was dead only when the raven landed on his shoulder.

(7) When you come to the top of the pass, you have reached the Priest's Leap, which marks the Cork-Kerry border. The name seems to have its origin in the penal times, about the seventeenth century. Then it was strictly forbidden to practise the Roman Catholic religion, under pain of death. Many of the priests of the time flouted this law by saying mass in secret in isolated locations, usually using an outcrop of rock as an altar. However, the law of the time persistently sought out these renegade priests and it was during such a foray that a local priest evaded capture by escaping into this glen. Folklore has it that as he neared the high pass he managed to lose his captors by leaping with his horse from the top of the glen across to the other side of Bantry Bay. The hoof prints of the horse are said to be discernible on a rock at the top. Additionally, when the horse landed on the other side, similar marks were made on another rock. A plaque to commemorate this amazing feat has been erected at the landing spot near the legendary marked stone, and it can be seen on the left-hand side of the road between Ballylickey and Bantry.

The walk finishes here, but before turning back it provides a wonderful opportunity to take in the surrounding views. Down the other side of the mountain runs the Sheen river that flows into Kenmare Bay. Beyond, the high mountains of Kerry dominate the landscape as they run westwards along the peninsula of Iveragh and out to Caherdaniel. Turning around and looking back down over the West Cork countryside, many of the areas where the walks in this book are located can be seen. To your right and behind the ridge of the glen, is the village of Glengarriff with its remnant *oak woods*. Some of the peaks of the Caha Mountains can also be seen protruding above the ridge as they run out to the sea near Allihies. Southwards from these mountains and across the waters of Bantry Bay, is the peninsula of Kilcrohane. Behind this lies the peninsula of Mizen, the two round domes of the tracking station on Mount Gabriel visible in the distance. Straight in front of you, at the edge of the land horizon, is the rounded hill of Knockomagh Mountain that overlooks Lough Hyne. Away to your left and still on the coastline, sits the demesne of Castle Freke.

## OPTION

To be attempted in clear weather only, when there is little risk of low cloud descending on the mountain top.

(8) Having arrived at the top of the pass and with Kerry stretching away to distant mountain peaks in front of you, go to your RIGHT. Cross the boggy heath towards the rocky escarpment visible ahead. This is the more difficult part of the climb to the summit, giving way to more open and undulating heath once it has been negotiated. But you should find no great difficulty in negotiating the rocks. Amongst the clefts of rock you may spot the uncommon *stag's horn clubmoss* which is actually a member of the fern family.

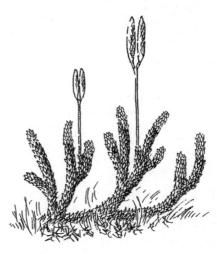

Stag's horn clubmoss is found only in damp wet moors and on high cliffs. Its characteristic spore-producing head is the reason for its name.

(9) Having come over the top of the rocks you will soon see the small upland lake, Lough Boy, in front of you. Further down to the right is the much larger Curramore Lough which in recent times has been dammed by the Electricity Supply Board in order to harness its power.

(10) Head for the LEFT-hand side of Lough Boy, crossing the sheep wire fence carefully at a strong point. The margins of these mountain loughs are usually surrounded by thick growths of *sphagnum moss* that have grown out over the deeper water. Thus the edges can be deceptive and should be approached with care. Even up here you will spot the slender bodies of small *damselflies* like the light coloured *common blue*. However it is the seldom-seen giant *aeshna dragonflies* which inhabit these boggy regions that are most impressive – they are my favourite insect. As big as the palm of your hand, they can be quite startling when first encountered, buzzing past at high speed, swirling and gyrating

The large aeshna dragonfly sticks to regular 'beats' when hunting other prey. If you can discover the beat, you can get a very good look at the large insect.

over your head as they chase other insects. They are totally harmless and if you stay very still you may be rewarded with one of them landing on your sleeve, a rare opportunity to see these rainbow-coloured creatures close up. Normally confined to the upland boggy regions they are rarely seen in the lowlands, thus they too are becoming another threatened species as the uplands are being destroyed beneath the barren blankets of commercial evergreen trees.

(11) Leaving the lough behind you, the top of Knockboy is visible and it is a simple walk up the turfy heath to its summit. Another sheep wire fence will have to be crossed. There is a good selection of different *heather* species about its rounded peak which come into bloom towards the end of the summer. Look for the strong purples of the *common purple heather*, and the delicate pinks of *ling heather*. There is a third

Heathers at first glance all look the same, but with closer examination of the leaves you can distinguish their tell-tale features – left to right: purple heather, ling, cross-leaved heath.

90

type, very similar in colour to ling, but this is the *crossed-leaved heath*. It is distinguishable by its tiny leaves arranged in a crossed foursome up along the stem.

(12) At the top of Knockboy is a concrete pillar that marks its highest point. If you stand on the northern side of this pillar (left, as you approach), you are in Kerry. While on its southern (right) side, you are standing in Cork. From here you now have an excellent view over the entire region. Standing with the pillar at your back and with Kerry on your left and Cork on your right you are looking down over the Borlin Valley. Beyond it are the Shehy Mountains, and the high point straight in front is Conigar Mountain. This towers above Gougane Barra and the issuing river Lee that flows through the Gearagh and on to Cork city. Away to the north-west, on your left, is Ireland's highest mountain, Carrauntoohil, poking up above the rest of the Macgillycuddy Reek Mountains that surround Killarney. The layout of the dense topography of mountains is enchanting – full of expansive moors and high-cliffed peaks that tower above the maze of twisted and half-hidden valleys. It is not hard to imagine why this southern region was the stronghold of the last *golden eagles*, who had their eyrie amongst the high ledges of Conigar above Gougane Barra. Leaving the summit, return by the same route.

# 9 – Glengarriff

WHEN LOOKING AT THE IRISH LANDSCAPE, most people imagine it as a country of open green fields and barren mountain tracks that have always been there and that typify its true nature. There was never a greater misconception. Very few people appreciate the magnitude of the transformation that occurred in the last two centuries. Ireland was originally a land of dense oak forest that up to the 1700s still cloaked the river valleys and mountain slopes. Here the wild wolf ran free and the eagles soared over their extensive domains of jungle-like wilderness.

In the subsequent two hundred years practically every single bit of native aboriginal forest vanished, recklessly plundered to the point of no return by the insatiable demands of a greedy and reckless humanity. Only a few ragged remnants of the original forests now remain, some of which are located in the more remote and inaccessible regions of the West Cork mountains. In Glengarriff, trapped within a rugged valley that stretches to the waters of Bantry Bay, there is an oak wood that has existed continually since its first appearance ten thousand years ago.

Completely sheltered by the Caha Mountains to the north, it is free from the effects of icy winds, while its coastal fringes are washed by the northern limit of the warming and moist Gulf Stream. These two factors together are responsible for producing woods of considerable luxuriance, full of moisture-loving mosses and ferns as well as plants of warmer climes. Thus we get rare filmy ferns covering the shady, woodland rocks, Irish spurge carpeting woodland floors, and the Mediterranean strawberry tree clambering through to the upper tree canopy – all indicative species that point to the wood's great age. However, the reason for the forest's survival today is not due to any scientific wonder but rather to the fact that it became part of an old eighteenth-century demesne belonging to the Earls of Bantry, and was kept for the hunting and recreational pursuits of the then ruling classes, after they had butchered all the rest. Unfortunately, since their departure, the woods have been extensively abused by the less well endowed who in their narrow-minded ignorance identify the area with the 'house of the planter', not realising that it was here long before even we ourselves arrived.

Happily, since the area is once again being appreciated for its romantic beauty and tourism value, more care is now being extended to its protection and maintenance. Hopefully we will not be as shortsighted as we have been in the past, and in developing it will not repeat those mistakes that interfere with its natural development in such a way as to precipitate its final extinction. Long may it outlive us.

## WALK DESCRIPTION

LOCATION: The walk is located in the woods above the town of Glengarriff. Travel along the Glengarriff-Kenmare road for 0.5ml/0.8km and enter the wood through the stone and timber walled gates, on your LEFT. The open gate is flanked by a picturesque lodge house built of cut stone. On entering, follow the track for about 200m to the carpark.

TERRAIN: A delightful walk along the empty by-roads and woodland nature trails that weave their way through the forested hills. It is a walk that is accessible to everyone and can be performed in any type of weather, with no difficulties being experienced along the good-quality green roads.

FEATURES: Oak and coniferous woods; woodland paths; Fine views over the forested valley, mountains and Glengarriff harbour, riverside walks with cascades; fabulous mountain heath; country by-roads;

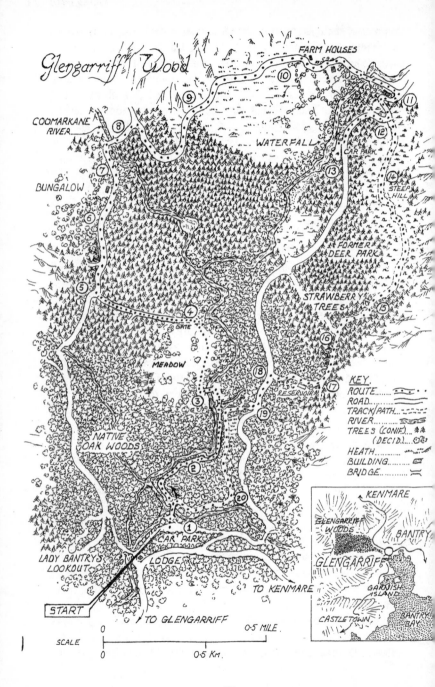

Glengarriff Wood

FARM HOUSES

COOMARKANE RIVER

WATERFALL

BUNGALOW

FORMER DEER PARK

STRAWBERRY TREES

MEADOW

GATE

RESERVOIR

NATIVE OAK WOODS

CAR PARK

LADY BANTRY'S LOOKOUT

LODGE

START

TO KENMARE

TO GLENGARRIFF

CAR PARK

STEEP HILL

KEY.
ROUTE ........
ROAD ..........
TRACK/PATH ...
RIVER .........
TREES (CONIF.) ...
       (DECID.) ...
HEATH .........
BUILDING .......
BRIDGE .......

KENMARE
GLENGARRIFF WOODS
BANTRY
GLENGARRIFF
GARNISH ISLAND
CASTLETOWN
BANTRY BAY

SCALE
0        0·5 MILE
0        0·5 KM.

94

strawberry trees; geological features.

LENGTH: 5 ml/8km.

TIME: 3 hours.

EQUIPMENT: Casual walking shoes.

## WALK OUTLINE

(1) On arriving at the carpark, walk across the grass lawn, cross the timber footbridge and go to the LEFT. The surrounding parklands were maintained by the Earls of Bantry in the eighteenth century. The enchanted wooded avenues once led to a romantic fairytale cottage, hidden on an island in the river in the depths of the forest. This had a thatched roof, sweeping, curved eaves, rustic verandas and Gothic tracery windows, fit for any Grimm's fairytale. Like the Earls themselves, the original cottage is now gone, having caught fire and burnt to the ground early in the last century.

(2) Follow the riverside path up through the trees. The richness of the woods is apparent in the moss-covered trees and rocks as well as the dense ground flora. *Polypody ferns* drip from the oak branches, while *frothens*, *heather* and *buckler ferns* clutter the ground around the tree trunks. A closer look at some of the shaded rocks will expose the rare *filmy fern*, a small moss-like plant that grows well in the warm and moist conditions of the south-west. In early May and June, the best months to observe the real glory of the indigenous West Cork plants, *Irish spurge* will be sporting its green-domed tufts on the woodland floor, while thin, red-stemmed spikes of tiny white flowers, rising from a circular rosette of leaves, identify the characteristic *kidney saxifrage*. These are plants that are rarely found outside the mountainous areas of the south-west, growing here with a vigour that is not matched anywhere on the island.

(3) The path leads up to a footbridge, after which there is a second bridge with a sign for the 'Big Meadow Trail'. Here go to the LEFT over the bridge and then cross over a third footbridge where you go to the RIGHT. Following the riverside path upstream, it eventually leads out onto a more open meadow. Now retained as a wild-flower meadow, little disturbance is exacted on the these fields, other than light grazing. This is a very sheltered area and clearly illustrates why so many eighteenth-century ruling families developed extensive tropical gardens here.

    Nearby Garnish Island is the crowning jewel of such efforts. At the

The Irish spurge is a member of the Lusitanian flora so characteristic of West Cork.

turn of the century, the island was planted with a fabulous collection of tropical plants, including representative samples from New Zealand, China, South America and Asia, all of which thrive in the frost-free climate of Glengarriff.

(4) On arriving at the other side of the meadow, a timber barricade with a stile is met. Pass through and go to the LEFT. Follow the track into the woods where, in spring, the white *lesser celandines* and yellow *anemones* spill from the woods onto the track side. Many tall oak trees line the route and these are decorated with lush growths of *ivy* and *moss* that provide rich feeding grounds and nesting sites for a multitude of woodland birds. Keep your eyes open for the mottled *tree-creeper* and the dozens of song birds that are constantly foraging through the fertile tree canopy. You should also stand a good chance of seeing the pink and blue-coloured *jay*, as Glengarriff is one of the strongholds of this woodland bird. In fact, as many as four hundred different types of organism depend on the oak tree for their survival, while conifers support less than a handful.

(5) As you proceed, a track will join in on the left, but ignore it. Instead keep on STRAIGHT until you arrive at a tarred road, through a timber gate with a stile. Here go to the RIGHT.

Along the way the remains of a clear-felled coniferous forest lines the route, very sterile when compared to the deciduous woods left behind. Some native trees have managed to find a foot-hold along the verges of the plantation; in this case they are mostly *silver birch* and *alder* which can tolerate the wetter soil. These native trees are also the food source of the *redpoll* and you may be lucky to spot some of these birds with their red crowns as they flit among the seed-heads, especially in autumn. Dark conifers flank the route on both sides – which may be a bit of a nuisance during the summer heat as they give shelter to irritating midges. The tiny, though harmless bites of these minute flies can cause the most annoying itch, driving one almost to despair. However, I have found that a twig of pine-scented *bog myrtle* if constantly fanned about the face is handy for keeping them at bay, while the sweet scent of lemon balm oil if rubbed to the skin stops them from biting for up to fifteen minutes – thus it needs repeated application!

(6) Eventually, the oak woods return and you pass a bungalow on your left. In mid-summer the rich aroma of *honeysuckle* wafts from the hedgerows, identifiable by its trailing stems and clusters of yellow, trumpet-shaped flowers. The complexity of associations that occur between different forms of woodland wildlife is well illustrated in the leaves of this plant. With a little searching, you should be able to find some of the honeysuckle leaves that have a delicate tracery of white winding lines through the leaf blade. This coil of lines is formed by the burrowing of the tiny *leaf-miner*. Hatched from an egg impregnated within the leaf tissues, the grub eats its way through the thin leaf, getting fatter as it burrows, and so too does the tunnel. Hold such a leaf up to the light and you should be able to see the small insect inside. A tiny animal, but very much a part of the woodland ecosystem. The leaf-miner depends totally on the honeysuckle for its way of life, so that without the host plant the insect could not exist.

(7) The rumblings of the Coomarkane river should shortly be heard ahead. It flanks the road on the right-hand side, as it pours down over rocky cascades and through crystalline pools that are overhung with giant *emperor*

Honeysuckle with leaf miner in its leaf. The plant is recognised by its rich sweet smell and yellow-red flowers.

97

*ferns*. An interesting spot to take a break. Watch the rocky stones beside the river for the black, white chested *dipper*. This bird can fly underwater! It chases the larvae of mayflies, caddisflies and stoneflies that hide beneath the stones. Pushing itself through the strong currents by beating its wings, it swims through the water with amazing agility. Periodically it pops out onto a rock with another mouthful and shakes the water from its water-repellent feathers before nose-diving back in. The Irish dipper is slightly different from the European and British race, thus it represents a separate and endemic sub-species unique to Ireland.

(8) The road follows the river upstream and crosses by a bridge, back into the coniferous woods. Within the wood, an open clearing is soon met, where there is a Y-junction. Go RIGHT. The road left leads into a dead-end valley out of which the Coomarkane river flows. This is a high-cliffed coomb where wild *goats* can be seen clambering about the precipitous walls in search of elusive tussocks of sweet grass. This is one of those enchanting valleys that calls you in, definitely a place worth exploring another day.

(9) Passing through the *conifers*, wild and beautiful tracts of heathland

open up on your left. This is frequently punctured by the rounded bones of old red sandstone rocks that protrude like a sea of islands across the wild expanses of *purple moor-grass*. Looking up to the higher hills you may recognise the characteristic terraced pleats of the layers of sandstone. These illustrate clearly the warping effect that occurred as these mountains were forced upwards over 250 million years ago by the Armorican or Hercynian movements. The heathland is festooned with the beautiful deep violet flowers of the endemic *butterwort* during the months of May and June. Water-logged pockets are full of the sticky, hairy-leaved *sundew*, also an insect-eater. In July and August numerous butterflies will be seen moving about in the bright sunshine. The orange-brown *large heath* butterfly may be spotted here, a generally rarer inhabitant of the bogs and heaths. It feeds on the white *cotton grass* that carpets the bogs in blankets of white during May and June.

(10) Gradually the bogs give way to some picturesque farm meadows of hilly knolls and hedgerows lined with trees. These surround the farm buildings of stone near the roadside track. In early summer this is a good area to hear the call of the male *cuckoo*, even if you don't spot it, as it tries to attract females. Plenty of *hedge sparrows* will guarantee ample hosts for the cuckoo hen as she moves from nest to nest depositing an egg in each. Along the hedgerows keep an eye out too for the *small copper butterfly* as it lays its eggs on the leaves of *docks* and *sorrel*.

(11) Continue on through the oak-wooded road, crossing the bridge over the Glengarriff river to arrive at a T-junction. Go RIGHT. The road soon passes a stone house on your right and then goes through a felled coniferous plantation.

(12) Within the felled *coniferous wood* and on a bend you should notice a forest track with a timber gate on your LEFT. This will be the direction of our route, but before entering the woods you may first like to visit the cascades on the river that are just around the corner by the carpark.

The orange-coloured small copper is frequently seen along flowery banks and small meadows.

(13) At the cascades there are some

picnic tables available, thus it is a good spot to rest, with many paths leading into the woods and around the river bank. This can be rather busy during the summer season, but if you are here in either autumn, winter or spring you will have the entire place to yourself. It is also a good location to see *kingfishers*, *otters* and *stoats* if you have the patience to sit around quietly for a while.

(12) Retrace your steps back to the forest track at point (12). The track is now on your RIGHT. Pass through the timber stile to enter the *coniferous wood* and follow the track up through what was originally the deer park.

(14) Much of this part of the original oak forest was cut earlier this century when the estate passed to the state and became subsequently planted with conifers. However many of the indigenous plants managed to survive, especially in the higher parts of the glen where disturbance was diminished.

(15) Within the woods a steep incline leads one up to the higher hills. Felled recently, there are good vistas available. One can see some fine examples of the rarer *strawberry tree* (or *arbutus*) that make the trek worthwhile. Where the road levels out on top, watch for a small bend on the track. Below the track on your right is a timber seat, while on your left there is a rocky outcrop. Just about here, both on the left and right hand sides, are a number of strawberry trees. These are more akin to a large shrub than a mighty tree, and have a reddish bark and small evergreen leaves similar to the *rhododendron* that make it hard to distinguish at first sight, especially in summer as it does not flower until autumn. Then, during the months of November and December, it is unmistakable with its bright red berries hanging from the upper branches like perfect round strawberries. The plant is a member of the unusual Lusitanian group found in the south-west of Ireland, even though it is more native to the shores of the Mediterranean. Its main significance however is not just in its rarity here in Ireland but more in the fact that it represents the old order that existed in the country before the demise of the forests. Thus its presence here in Glengarriff indicates that some remnant of the former forest is still surviving in the district, despite much of the damage that has been inflicted by commercial planting and illegal felling of the oaks.

(16) Continuing on along the road another track branches off to the right, but ignore this and keep going straight on.

(17) Soon afterwards a Y-junction is reached, with a sign for the 'Eshnamucky Walk'. Go RIGHT, heading downhill along the track, which is rather rough and weather-torn – thus it will be muddy during wet weather. Mixed in with the *oaks* are some older *Scots pine*, which are also probable remnants of the former native forest. Lower down, the trees begin to become

The strawberry tree's characteristic warty red fruits are unmistakable in late Autumn – but they are not edible.

enveloped in thickets of *rhododendron*, an alien species that was introduced from Portugal and the Middle East in the last century by the wealthy landlords of the time. Sadly the plant left its mark on these woods in a way they could not have imagined. Obsessed with the desire for order and beauty in all things, the late Victorian gentry sought to further enhance the appearance of their estates with exotic varieties of shrubs. Into the very structure of the aboriginal forest they carved elaborate paths and avenues that allowed them to experience the delight of these wonderful wooded hills. Exotic shrubs lined the paths that led to cascades, high vista points and the beautiful cottage orne, but none of these exotics has been more devastating than the evergreen *rhododendron*. A native of warmer climes, it has thrived in the mini-tropical climate of West Cork. Spreading like a plague through the woods for the last hundred years, it has snuffed out the entire forest floor in an impenetrable tangle of inter-twining branches. It blocks out all light from the ground throughout the entire year, and all native ground flora has been completely exterminated. The leaves resist decay and cannot be eaten by animals and the branches offer little protection for nesting. *Rhododendron* when established drastically reduces the wildlife potential of the habitat.

As of 1998, vast amounts of the rhododendron has been removed. This can look a bit drastic at first, but it has given new life to the forests. Look for the amount of regeneration of young *oaks* that is taking place. The Department of Wild Life are to be greatly commended on their efforts to restore the ancient woodlands, as are voluntary groups like the

Irish Wildlife Trust, which provides voluntary support of environmentalists from around the world, through its 'Groundwork' programme. This is an organisation very well worth supporting.

(18) At the bottom of the hill the track passes through a stile and joins back with the tarred roadway again. Go LEFT. A few cars will be met here, so do walk with care. The roadway is overhung with mighty *oaks* that tower above the thickets of *rhododendron*, which, despite the problems they cause, are quite impressive in June when their large pink and red flowers come into bloom turning the roadside into a tropical garden.

(19). After a few bends in the roadway a small picnic site is reached on the RIGHT. This has a number of seats and a signpost for a river side walk. Turn in to the site and follow the riverside walk which goes up a number of stone steps on the LEFT of the large rock. The footpath winds its way through the thickets of rhododendron and past some boggy heath. The bog is a small patch of wilderness that has not been planted, and thus supports a good variety of wetland flowers in summer.

(20) Further on the path comes close to the river and leads on to an excellent example of the more natural and open forest. Around here you should be able to see *tree creepers* scrambling up the tree trunks in search of insects, and *red squirrels* scurrying about the branches. The fine trees are well spaced, leaving plenty of room for the natural woodland flowers and shrubs to develop. In March and April rich blankets of the white-petalled *wood anemone* grow before the appearance of the oak-leaf canopy. In October and November the deep leaf-fall covers the woodland floor and a variety of attractive *fungi* may be found pushing up through the golden-brown leaves.

(1) Keep close to the riverside path until you meet a timber bridge on your LEFT. CROSS the bridge to arrive back in the carpark.

# 10 – Allihies

ENCIRCLED AND ENCLOSED by the gaping, raw walls of hungry and mountainous peaks, the romantic hamlet of Allihies sits teetering on the edge of a pounding ocean surf. Hidden recluse-like at the end of the Beara Peninsula, this small farming community nestles within the protruding arms of the Slieve Miskish Mountains in the little-known Ballydonegan Bay. So isolated is this area of coastline, you could be forgiven for feeling you were on an island. In this lies its incredible beauty. The peace and pleasure of its golden beach, rugged cliffs, and hedgerowed farms, protected from the pollution of the outside world by the fortress walls of the surrounding rocky masses, make one want to keep this little-known gem of West Cork secret.

Its wild, forlorn appearance is accentuated by the total absence of trees, a fact that points to the difficulty experienced in extracting a living from such tough and exposed terrain. However, hardship was not always the norm, as back in the last century the area was a thriving mining location, where copper ore was extracted from the sterile hills. The legacy of this activity still lies scattered across the surrounding landscape. Precarious mine shafts litter the many meadows, while old and crumbling chimneys poke silently from the mountain slopes. Their noisy whirring and belching smoke are now gone, along with the copper vein. And, of course, gone too are the last of the trees, sacrificed to the furnaces that continually pumped water from the mines. Hopefully, like once before, the community will realise that its present assets lie at their feet too, but in a less devastating form than that of the mines. By maintaining the area's unspoiled beauty, the charm of its solitude, the tranquillity of its many paths and by-roads and the romance engendered by its small farm holdings, they will attract the more discerning tourist that is increasingly being drawn to our shores. To walk the wave-lashed coastline on a cold, crisp autumnal day or to follow abandoned tracks over mountain peaks that throw out map-like views of the surrounding coast, gives a sense of freedom and exhilaration that is difficult to find anywhere else in Europe.

## WALK DESCRIPTION

LOCATION: Situated at the end of the Beara peninsula in the village of Allihies, 10ml/16km from Castletown Bearhaven. It can be approached from either the Kenmare or the Glengarriff side.

TERRAIN: Mostly along old mountain tracks and bog roads, but the middle of the walk does include a strenuous trek across open moorland without any path. Therefore the complete walk is not suitable for very young children or the less fit and should be attempted in fine weather only. However the mountain tracks at the start and the end of the route are ideal one-way walks for all types.

LENGTH: 7ml/11km.

TIME: 4 hours.

FEATURES: Rocky mountain heath; old copper mines; incredible views of Kenmare Bay and Bantry Bay as well as some coastal islands; mountain bogs and turf-cutting; standing stones; quiet country lanes; beach.

EQUIPMENT: Good walking shoes with waterproof boots for the higher moors. Windproof jacket and jumper during cooler weather, thus an advantage to bring a knapsack. NO DOGS.

## WALK OUTLINE

(1) The walk starts in the village of Allihies where reputedly the first people to arrive in Ireland, the legendary Milesians, first landed over four thousand years ago, appearing out of the Atlantic mists in the west.

Allihies

SCALE

0  0.5 Km.  0.5 MILE

KNOCKDURA

KNOCKGOUR

MAST

SHEEP PEN

GALLAUNS

GALLAUN

BEARHAVEN
COPPER
MINES

ALLIHIES

TENNIS
COURT

START

CAMINCHES RIVER

KEY:
ROUTE ........
ROAD ............
TRACK ..........
MINE .............
CHIMNEY .......
BEACH .........

COULAGH
BAY

GLENGARRIFF

BALLY
DONEGAN
BAY

ALLIHIES

CASTLETOWN
BERE

DURSEY IS.

105

(2) Leaving the village from its top end, pass the tennis courts on your left and head for the mountains. You arrive immediately at a fork in the road. Go RIGHT at the fork and travel on for a few hundred metres until you pass another road going back towards the village on your right. Ignore this turn-off, watching instead for the untidy open space on your left and just beyond the junction. This is the entrance to the copper mines.

(3) Swing LEFT onto the old road that leads up to the copper mines in the hills above. These were discovered by a Colonel Hall way back in 1810, to finally fade away around 1930. They are old and unsafe if you approach too closely. Follow the track upwards, winding your way between the bare rocks and abandoned mine shafts. The shafts are quite numerous, but being well fenced-off, pose no danger if not interfered with, so keep to the path.

(4) Shortly you will pass another lane to your left – ignore it and continue on up STRAIGHT. Above you can be seen the ominous ruins of one of the old chimney stacks which helped pump water out of the catacomb of tunnels riddling these mountain slopes under your feet. Long forsaken, the stack remains to look down hauntingly on the village below. As you ramble upwards, an abandoned reservoir, drained of its water and identifiable by the remaining stone barricade, skirts the roadside on your right. It now crumbles before the slow return of wild nature as the stones become recolonised with *moss* and *fern*, the water-logged pools with *rush* and *sedge* that support returning moorland insects and act as small sanctuaries for *newt* and *frog*. A heartening sight when one ponders on the devastation the mines must have had on the landscape as well as on the people that were compelled to slave in them over 150 years ago, with even children having to work there.

(5) Swinging to the left as you approach the refurbished old mine-house entrance, you shortly come within striking distance of the chimney stack and a clutter of mine shafts. Keep your distance from these; they are fenced off for obvious reasons. Some plummet all the way to sea level and are enough to make the hair stand on the back of your neck. Remember, the old pumps no longer work, so they are full of water, are in a bad state of decay and surrounded by slippery and loose rocks. It is said that the workers used to descend these in crude ladders, climbing down several hundreds of feet to get at the valuable ore in the caverns below. Beneath, the maze of tunnels burrow all the way through the

Many of the tunnels and shafts are in a poor state of decay
– more reminiscent of hell!

mountains to exit on the other side, while some are said to go out under the sea. I got the chance to enter them as a boy and can only describe the experience as nightmarish, with black abysses opening up, full of stinking green water that plummeted down several hundred feet. The shafts soar upwards through the mountains giving lonesome and distant views of the sky. Gigantic piles of rock litter the tunnels from roof cave-ins, and rotting stakes support sagging roofs, ready to crack at any moment. Best to keep well away!

(6) Continue on up the track that soon swings to the right around the chimney stack. Looking back, a panoramic view of the bay has opened up behind you, its fine golden beach shining bright in the summer sunshine. The crystal-grained sand is supposed to have been formed

from the outwashings of the mine. Away to your right is the bleached peninsula of Cod's Head, made of granite from the volcanoes that existed here millions of years ago, which also deposited the copper. While to the left are the sandstone, heather-clad hills of Garnish Point behind which hides Dursey Island. This island is accessible by a fearsome cablecar ride across a racing, high cliffed sound and is another incredible place to walk. To the right of Garnish Point can be seen the Bull Rock and the Cow Rock, the former having a lighthouse.

(7) Continue on UP the track. As you near the top, you leave the mines behind you and the moors become a safe place to cross. All the mine shafts are down below, scattered about the farms and along the roadside fields. Presently, as you reach the road's summit – and if you are lucky to get a fine clear day – the vista that opens up before you of the Iveragh Peninsula and Kenmare Bay is stunning. Across the wide expanse of water the lofty peaks of the Kerry Reeks pierce the sky like some strange land of pyramids, their bases rising straight out of the blue ocean.

(8) Head straight for the bend in the road that disappears around the side of the mountain ahead. Going around the bend, proceed for about 30m or 40m and go RIGHT, scrambling up across the rocky heathland, making for the first high peak. But if you have first reached a small lay-by on your right you have gone too far. The track has a wire fence on its left, from which good views of the valley running down to Coulagh Bay can be had. This descends down towards the village of Eyries, passing the mine tunnels that emerge out on this side.

(9) Having crossed the heath and arriving on top of the first peak, the island of Dursey can be made out at the end of the Beara Peninsula, its raw hump of thin heath denuded by the blast of winter gales and the hand of the tree-cutter. However, like up here the subsequent development of bogs has thrown out its own array of wild species. Underfoot you will trample on the common yellow *tormentil* that likes the drier parts of the heath, while the strange insect-eating *sundews* prefer the wetter callows where they can catch the emerging insects that spend their larval stages in the wet muds. You may be lucky and spot the extremely rare *Mediterranean heath*, with its delicate pink flowers on one side of the stem, now found only in a small few undisturbed patches of bog on the western seaboard. Additionally you may come across other rarities like *blue-eyed grass*, a flower of American origin or the *Alpine lady's-mantle*. Please do not be tempted to pick these, but guard

their location jealously if you find them and report it to the Botanic Gardens, Dublin, where all plant records are kept. Many of our rare species were practically wiped out by eccentric Victorian plant collectors in the nineteenth century, many to be used as bookmarks and other such trivial things. If more people realised that finding a healthy population of such species is all that is needed in a lot of cases to protect a particularly threatened habitat, the future of rare species would be much safer.

(10) Looking down on Allihies from the peak, you must now turn LEFT towards the next peak. But as this is a rocky and awkward route to follow it is better to stay to the left of the peak itself and walk along the gentle slope behind it. As you proceed keep the shoreline around Coulagh Bay on your left in view at all times and the higher undulating ridge above you and to your right, until you come to an obvious bend in the mountain range.

The delicate yellow petals of the common tormentil are a frequent sight on all moors and heaths.

(11) After two kilometres, turn RIGHT up along the smooth slope that leads to the highest of these peaks, which is Knockoura. Keep the sheep-wire fence to your right and make for the top. As you rise up towards the rounded summit of turf and heather, the bay around Allihies comes back into view. It is in thick heather like this that the *skylarks* dwell, finding refuge from patrolling *kestrels* and *merlins*. The purple flowers are rich in nectar, and so they draw many *moths, flies* and *bumble bees*, the latter filling the moors with their buzzing drone on calm summer days. From June onwards a migrant butterfly, the *painted lady*, will begin to appear, first reaching land on the south-western peninsulas after crossing from France. One unusual bird you will surely notice is what at first appears to be a crow – but look and listen again. This is the red-beaked and red-legged *chough*, that has a very characteristic voice. This bird is a rarity over much of the country and is practically extinct in Europe. It lives around the steep, rocky coastline of Ireland, often kiting over adjacent moors in search of food.

(12) On reaching the top of Knockoura you will notice that turf-cutting is taking place. Thus there is a bog road to be found which runs straight ahead along the ridge apex towards the large masts at the other end. Follow this track STRAIGHT AHEAD. To your left, the mountains of the peninsula itself can now be seen running inland and looking quite impressive. They hide a wealth of crannied valleys that beckon one to explore. Here nature is master, as very little human life dwells in this high and inhospitable terrain. And wherever the heather has been allowed to dominate you will be sure to find healthy communities surviving, all well suited to the mountainous habitat, whether it be the swift-sprinting *hare* or the large numbers of *stonechats* that find ample supplies of shelter and food in this short shrub-like plant.

(13) As you approach the ridge's end you will pass the masts on your right after which the track also swings around to the right. From up here, better and better vistas of Bantry Bay unfold along the route. Across the bay itself is the rocky spine of the Kilcrohane Peninsula. To your left, Bear Island, off-shore from Castletown Bere. Just down below you, again on the left, are the more sheltered farms with their hedgerow trees and coniferous woods. Thus they are able to support a greater concentration of song-birds than the exposed fields of Allihies.

(14) Follow the track DOWN, passing the lane on the right which leads back up to the masts. As the track winds its way downward through several hair-pin bends, you finally pass through a gate to reach the open meadows. Down here, the more sterile, wild *rush* replaces the richer *heather,* being better suited to the soggy wet soil fed by mountain springs. Extensive sheep-grazing inhibits natural regeneration while aiding the spread of less edible forms of plants like the *mat grass*. Thus these lower fields can be rather barren in contrast to the wealth of wildlife found in the higher, heather-clad moors above.

The spike-like head of the yellow bog asphodel occurs frequently in boggy fields rather than on the more exposed high moors.

(15) The track eventually joins another grass-covered one coming up from Castletown on your left, just beyond a concrete sheep pen. Go to the RIGHT. You should also notice the two standing stones in the heathery field sloping down in front of you before you turn to the right. These are quite accessible across the short growth of *heather* and *dwarf autumn gorse*, amongst which the yellow *bog asphodel* may be found.

(16) As the road runs down to the valley, the better-drained fields return. In one of these, down below you on your right, sits another standing stone – but a bit more unusual in that it is white, with a lot of crystalline marble.

(17) The track eventually develops into a tarred road. Follow it on DOWNHILL until a T-junction is met and go LEFT. Dozens of mine shafts litter the fields, their mouths coated in thickets of *bracken* and *furze*, as are the surrounding outcrops of rock. This is the highest the vegetation has been allowed to achieve with not a single native tree in sight to spread its seeds, except a few foreign *conifers*. Still, it suits the *wrens* that are frequently seen darting about the low cover and periodically uttering their tell-tale and click-like chirping which reaches its peak in winter, rather than in the more popular spring chorus.

(18) Presently you come to a Y-junction. Go to the RIGHT, following the sign for the youth hostel, which is written in Irish: An Oige.

(19) Soon afterwards, you come to a second Y-junction that has a sloping grass-covered island at its centre. Go to the RIGHT.

(20) The road almost immediately arrives at a third Y-junction. Take the RIGHT turn and follow it for about 0.5km down to the main road. Keep away from the unprotected mine shaft on the left-hand side of the road.

(21) On arriving at the T-junction, which is the main road, go to your RIGHT.

(22). After 100m a side road is met on the left. Take this LEFT turn and it will lead you down to the beach, which you can get onto by fording a small stream that runs through the strand on this side. If unable to cross the stream there are some stepping stones, up to your right, near the exit track. You should be able to cross these and then onto the beach with a bit of effort.

(23) Crossing the beach, if it is quiet, small waders can sometimes be seen probing the shoreline for food. These are usually *ringed plovers,* identifiable by their quick, running spurts. Out on the water the

conspicuous white *gannets* are a common sight in summer, plummeting arrow-like into the water after the shoals of small fish. They breed on Little Skellig, one of the two rocky outcrops visible out to sea on the right. This is the biggest gannet colony in Ireland, the birds flying up from the warm Atlantic waters off the coast of Africa each spring. Unfortunately their numbers are being affected by the miles of discarded fishing nets that are increasingly tossed overboard by some irresponsible fishing crews. Like immense snares, these plastic nets, which do not rot, are wreaking havoc with our marine life as many birds

The gannet has an excellent streamlined body that suits its way of life – forever plummeting off the coast into the sea in mighty splashes.

become entangled in them, ultimately to starve. Additionally, the beaches and coastline are becoming badly polluted by the tons of plastic that floats perpetually on the surface. The careless discarding of plastic refuse for the last twenty-five years is now beginning to take its toll. After the greenhouse effect and the ozone hole, the dying of the oceans is going to become the next major environmental catastrophe. You will not be able to avoid noticing the plastic on the beach, mixed in with the fragments of *kelp*, whose whip-like stems litter the upper tide level. Sadly some of this plastic has its origins far from the Irish coast, being transported here by ocean currents.

(24) Arriving at the other side of the beach, exit out onto the tarred road by the pier and go RIGHT. Pass the next narrow by-road on the left.

(25) Take the next LEFT turn when you come to the four-crossroads a little further on. This takes you back up to the village and your parked car.